CONCILIUM

Religion in the Seventies

CONCILIUM

Editorial Directors

Concilium 128 (8/1979): Ecumenism

CONFLICTS ABOUT THE HOLY SPIRIT

Edited by

Hans Küng
and
Jürgen Moltmann

THE SEABURY PRESS / NEW YORK

1979
The Seabury Press, 815 Second Avenue, New York, N.Y. 10017
ISBN: 0-8164-0129-2   0-8164-2035-1 (pbk.)

T. & T. Clark Ltd., 36 George Street, Edinburgh EH2 2LQ
ISBN: 0 567 30008 0 (pbk.)

Library of Congress Catalog Card Number: 79-92974
Printed in the United States of America

CONTENTS

Prologue

Dear Reader,

IF YOU read everything that is said in this number about the Holy Spirit, you will inevitably be struck by its disparate nature. It would in fact have been an easy task to make a whole number out of each of the four parts—one on the Son and the Spirit, another on the Word and the Spirit, a third on the Church's office and the Spirit and a fourth on spirits and the Spirit. What complex questions and what a variety of concerns—the concerns of the Eastern Orthodox Church and those of the Reformation, the concerns of Rome and those of the charismatic movement! But can they, in fact, be grouped under one heading?

Quite apart from the fact that there is only one number of *Concilium* devoted to ecumenism each year and not four, however, we are bound to ask whether the Holy Spirit is not above all one. Should we not try, especially now, after a period of so many secular controversies, to go beyond the frontiers of our own particular problem and look at other problems, in order to obtain a view of the whole problem, even though we may not be able to solve it? Should we not, in this way, attempt to become conscious of the relative nature of our own little individual or confessional spirit? This may be a way of learning something that is essential to our own understanding of the Spirit from others and thus gaining a deeper insight into what ultimately transcends all our ideas and concepts—the mysterious reality of the Holy Spirit who is at the same time the Spirit of God and Jesus Christ and whom no Church and no theology can ever have at their disposal.

What we could do and have in fact done is to provide authors belonging to the various churches—the Eastern Orthodox Church, the Protestant and the Free Churches, the Catholic Church and Roman Catholicism—with the opportunity to express the concerns of their own churches in complete freedom. (This freedom is by no means something that is accepted without question in all theological journals!) Not in all, but in almost all the contributions, theological commitment to the author's own position has, in a very refreshing way, been combined with an honest spirit of self-criticism. All the contributions, however, whether they come from the traditional countries of ecumenism, from Central Europe and North America, from the Greek or the Roman tradition or from Norway or Bulgaria, have this in common: they stimulate thought. This at least is the hope of the editorial directors of this review on ecumenism.

HANS KÜNG
JÜRGEN MOLTMANN

Eduard Schweizer

What is the Holy Spirit?
A Study in Biblical Theology

HOW CAN we distinguish the Holy Spirit from any other spirits there may be? This was the question already being asked by the Corinthians. Paul's answer—that he is present wherever Christ is acknowledged as Lord, and is therefore available for the benefit of all, for the building up of the Christian Community (1 Cor. 12:3, 7; 14:4f.)—soon ceased to be sufficient. Irenaeus already sees duly ordained bishops as guarantors of the Holy Spirit—a position definitively established by the Council of Trent. Over against this, the Reformation maintained the absolute inerrancy of Scripture down to the Hebrew pointing, while in protest against both churches all sorts of groups have sought for confirmation of the Spirit in the stirring of the individual heart. Where then is he?[1]

1. THE OLD TESTAMENT

At first Israel experienced the Spirit as a sinister, often actually evil, power, and for this reason there are only two references in the Old Testament to the 'holy' Spirit: Ps. 51:11 and Isa. 63:10f. Under his influence men can prophesy night and day until they fall to the ground naked and exhausted (1 Sam. 19:19-24), or be driven out into the mountains and thrown into ravines (2 Kings 2:16). Micah, however, dissociates himself from this view (3:5-8), and we find that wise political decisions (Gen. 41:38; Judg. 3:10; 6:34; 11:29; 1 Sam. 11:6; 16:13; 2 Sam. 23:2) as well as understanding and craftsmanship (Exod. 31:3; 35:31; Deut. 34:9; Job 32:8; Mal. 2:15) can be the gift of the Spirit. Therefore he only stands over against 'flesh' in cases where men rely on the flesh alone, instead of on God (Jer. 17:5; 2 Chron. 32:8), or perhaps on the Egyptians who still 'are men, and not God; and their horses are flesh, and not spirit' (Isa. 31:3). But it is precisely the (jealous, lying, lascivious) spirit of men that tempts them into these errors (Num. 5:14; Isa. 19:14; Hos. 4:12; 5:4).

Israel first experienced God's activity in history in the 'blast (equals spirit!) of his nostrils', the 'strong east wind (equals spirit!)', which dried up the sea (Exod. 14:21; 15:8-10). In this way they learned that God created the world through Word and Spirit (Gen. 1:2; Ps. 33:6), and that each springtime he brings it to life again (Ps. 147:18). All the life of his creation is none other than his Spirit, which he breathes out and breathes back in again when death occurs (Ps. 104:29f.; Job 34:14f.). The question, of course, is whether we recognise it. God's Spirit is indeed at work in his creation, but 'how small a whisper do we hear of him' (Job 26:13f.). 'Spirit' and 'Word' often occur together (2 Sam. 23:2; Ps. 33:6; 147:18; Isa. 59:21). The former stresses God's staggering, often inconceivable, aliveness; the latter, the fact that he wants to be recognised and known. Under the crushing experience of the Exile, Israel learns to set its hope on a new creation in which God's Spirit alone will be in control—as a storm of judgment, which destroys everything (Hos. 13:15), and as a refreshing wind, which turns the wilderness into an orchard (Isa. 32:15-18); for the very storm-Spirit of God, as he sweeps away all that is evil, is creating a pure and holy people (Isa. 4:4). Whoever calls upon God on 'the great and terrible day of the Lord' will be delivered and endowed with his Spirit (Joel 2). Then God will place his own Spirit in the heart of man, to destroy all evil and create a new heart in him (Ezek. 36:25-27; 39:28f.).

2. JUDAISM BETWEEN THE OLD AND NEW TESTAMENTS

Is it possible to continue to believe in the 'strangeness' of the Spirit, who imparts knowledge of God, when one can no longer construe all that is inexplicable as evidence of God's activity? Jewish scholars chose a combination of the 'protestant' and 'catholic' solutions: only the biblical prophets are guaranteed bearers of the Spirit, and only the one who has been properly ordained in an unbroken succession can interpret them, because this is the way in which the Spirit bestowed on Moses in passed on. In this way the radical 'otherness' of God's Spirit was preserved. Unfortunately the Spirit himself did not keep to the rules! The more men tried to restrict him to the biblical 'preserves' the more frequently it happened that prophets appeared who were not recognised and therefore could not be controlled and reminded of their limits, and who on that account fascinated people the more. Philo chose the 'charismatic' solution, saying that it is only when all human thought is eliminated that the Spirit can speak: 'I believed that I was moving in higher regions, through

God's imparting of his Spirit to my soul.' But biblical prophets have put forward very rational political and social solutions when under the influence of the Spirit, while many of those who have been 'Spirit-possessed' and no longer exercising their reason have been false prophets. The Qumran community looked for the guarantee of the Spirit in the verifiable miracle of fulfilment (Temple Scroll 61:2-5; Deut. 18:22; see also Ps. Clem. Hom. 2:6-11). But even in the case of the genuine prophet not everything is certain to be fulfilled (Jonah 3:10). Where are we then?

The activity of the Spirit in creation remained equally problematical. Those who were influenced by what at that time was modern natural science, and could no longer speak of angels opening the rain-tanks and simultaneously letting off thunder and lightning, thought of God's Spirit as a kind of electric current which, at different intensities, flowed through everything. But did not that make him an anonymous natural force, in which there was no longer any room for God's freedom? The hope of eternal life had at that time become fashionable. The scepticism of the Preacher—'Who knows whether the spirit of man goes upward and the spirit of the beast goes down to the earth?' (Eccl. 3:21)—did not find many echoes (cf. 2 Macc. 7:22f.; Wisd. of Sol. 1:13; 2:1, 23; 4:7, 10; 5:5, 15!). It was generally believed that there was a God-given spirit, peculiar to man, which left him at death and was kept in store ready to be united with a new body at the Resurrection. But does not that mean that the biblical way of looking at man as a unity has been lost in favour of a platonic separation of body and soul?

3. THE NEW TESTAMENT

1. *The Gospels*

Jesus himself spoke very little about the Spirit. He gave us neither a christology nor a pneumatology. Rather he *lived* in the Spirit as God's Son. Both Mark and Matthew felt the 'strangeness' of the Spirit so strongly that they speak almost exclusively of the Spirit living again in *Jesus.* According to Matt. 1:18 and Luke 1:35 the Creator Spirit is already at work even in his procreation. Yet (according to the new interpretation of the Baptist's announcement of the judge who will come in fire and storm) he will baptise his followers 'with the Holy Spirit' (Matt. 3:11, par.). Luke stresses already that the Spirit is not only at work in extraordinary miraculous happenings, but that he is given to all. Numbers 11:29 ('Would that all the Lord's people were prophets!') is fulfilled: the Spirit is *the* gift of God (Luke 11:13) to those who believe and obey (Acts 2:38; 5:32). While the first formulation of faith is not yet ascribed to him, the testimony to faith given by preaching certainly is (along with such passages as Acts 8:29; 10:19; 11:28, etc., see their 'normal' sequel in

Acts 9:31); for a community without a mission would no longer be the community of the Holy Spirit. Does Luke also think of a 'spirit' which survives death? Luke 8:55 and 23:46 may suggest that he does, but in Acts 20:10 he speaks only of 'life' coming back, and in 9:40 of the opening of the eyes, while according to Luke 24:37-39 'a spirit' is precisely what the Risen Lord is not. At all events the 'spirit' is not 'the person himself', and it is not really possible to base belief in an immortal soul on Luke.

2. *Paul*

Paul too refers to the 'signs and wonders' of the Spirit (Rom. 15:19; 1 Cor. 2:4; 1 Thess. 1:5). But the decisive wonder is something different: 'What no eye has seen, nor ear heard, nor the heart of man conceived . . . God has revealed to us through the Spirit'—that is, the Crucified One, a 'stumbling-block' and 'folly' then as today, even God's 'curse' (Deut. 21:22f.; Temple Scroll 64:12; Gal. 3:13), but to the believer the wisdom of God (1 Cor. 1:18—2:16). This strange law of God applies also to the disciples of Jesus: at the very moment of weakness God's power is present (2 Cor. 13:4; 12:10). For this reason Paul can no longer trust in the 'flesh', although it is part of God's good creation, and although there is a 'Christ according to the flesh' (Rom. 9:5). The opposite to 'flesh' is not a (human) 'spirit', but only God himself (1 Cor. 1:26; 2 Cor. 1:12; 10:4; 11:17f.; see Rom. 9:8; Gal. 4:23). Man is obliged to live 'in the flesh' but he must not conduct himself 'according to the flesh' (2 Cor. 10:3). When in fact he does so, the 'flesh' acquires power over him (as does alcohol over the person who comes to rely on it, though it can be used to cleanse wounds). Therefore it is not the bodily nature of man (sexuality, temper, greed for money) that constitutes 'flesh' in its most dangerous aspect, but rather the 'spiritual' side of it, its works of the law (Gal. 3:2, 5), its moral perfection (Phil. 3:3-7—'blameless' as to God's law!). The murderer is not often aware that all is not well with him; neither is the moralist, looking around on others. It was therefore Israel's particular calling to demonstrate to the world that man can fail God precisely at his religious high spots, and not simply when he becomes an animal. And it is just there that God's grace has broken in most radically (Rom. 5:20). In place of life 'according to the flesh' appears life created 'through the Spirit' (Phil. 3:3; Rom. 8:13f.; and notice the change of preposition in Gal. 4:23). Both life 'according to the flesh' and life 'through the Spirit' are expressed in 'works' (plural), which can be performed and enumerated, and which are 'plain'. Life 'through the Spirit' produces the 'fruit' of the Spirit, which, as it develops, brings life with all its light and shade into line with God (Gal. 5:19, 22), whose power is at work in the weak. So the Spirit becomes the Spirit of holiness (Rom. 15:16), and individuals, as well as the community, become his 'temple' (1 Cor. 6:19; 3:16). This is no new 'law', since 'where the Spirit of the Lord is, there is freedom' (2 Cor. 3:17), precisely because he bestows the wisdom necessary for making right decisions—decisions which do not 'lay restraint upon' others (1 Cor. 7:35, 40). This is only comprehensible because the decisive activity of the Spirit is to create openness towards God and at the same time towards one's fellow-men. He teaches us to pray (Gal. 4:6f.; Rom. 8:15-17); indeed he himself prays in us and so interprets our sighing, for which we cannot find the right words, in such a way that God can understand it (Rom. 8:26f.). Such a directing of our being to God frees us from the compulsion to interpret ourselves, and therefore gives us a heart open to others, the 'love of the Spirit' (Rom. 15:30). Love is the first of the Spirit's fruits (Gal. 5:22), the gift which embraces all the others and builds up the community (1 Cor. 13 comes between chapters 12 and 14, as Rom. 12:9a comes between verses 3-8 and 9b-13). Where the community is destroyed because it is thought that there is no room for the more conservative Peter alongside the more radical Paul and the more charismatic Apollos (1 Cor. 3:4, 17, 22), there God's Spirit is no longer present.

The activity of the Spirit in creation is of course presupposed, and for that reason not specifically mentioned in the New Testament. The new creation, which begins with the in-breaking of the Spirit in Jesus (Mark 1:9-11; Matt. 1:18; Luke 1:35), is so very much more important: the hymn in Col. 1:15-20 recognises that the first creation (in which the law of the survival of the fittest applies!) can only be recognised as God's creation in the light of the new creation in the resurrection of Jesus. This 'new creation in Christ' (2 Cor. 5:17; 'of the Spirit'—Titus 3:5) is, however, the Body of Christ, in which we are incorporated by the Spirit in baptism (1 Cor. 12:13). Here the prophecies of the new creation through the rippling streams of God's Spirit (Isa. 44:3; see 43:20) are fulfilled. Here the law of the survival of the weak applies (1 Cor. 12; 22f.).

This brings Paul to an insight which is important for succeeding millennia: that the peculiarity of the gift is no proof of its origin in God's Spirit. The same phenomena were to be found in paganism (1 Cor. 12:2). All that matters is whether through the gift Christ (and not perhaps one's own possession of the gift!) is recognised as Lord, and the whole community built up (verses 3, 7). Hence welfare work and administration (for which in the view of the Corinthians a broom or dinner-bell might be necessary, but not the Spirit—v. 29f.!) are just as much gifts of the Spirit as speaking with tongues (v. 28). Paul does indeed regard this latter gift highly, but not as highly as the service of others. All gifts are therefore 'supernatural' if the miracle of miracles truly happens, that God's grace reaches men through them and brings them to salvation. Therefore no 'ear', however much on one side it may be, should feel itself inferior to the 'eye', which, although it looks down on everything from above, should not feel superior to the 'hands' (which perhaps work in dirty dishwater) (1 Cor. 12:15-25).

For Paul too the Spirit operates in this world, not the world to come, but is a 'foretaste' of it, a 'downpayment' on it (Rom. 8:23; 2 Cor. 1:22; 5:5; Eph. 1:13f.; see Heb. 6:4f.). This very Spirit who knows all about the perfection to come is here in solidarity with the whole creation, because he suffers deeply with it in its anguish (Rom. 8:22f.). He sets us free from the misguided zeal which wants to live already with the Spirit in heaven and forget the earth and its sufferings. Already in pre-Pauline thought the Spirit is seen as at work in the resurrection of Jesus (Rom. 1:4; see 1 Tim. 3:16; 1 Pet. 3:18), and for Paul the Risen Christ is a 'life-giving spirit' who bestows the 'spiritual' resurrection body (1 Cor. 15:44-49) which our human minds cannot conceive of. That will happen one day 'through his Spirit which dwells in' us (Rom. 8:11). It can even be said, if we look at things from God's side, that the believer has already woken up to this new life (Col. 2:12). In Rom. 6:1-11, however, Paul avoids making such a statement, to guard against all misguided zeal, because, although we have indeed died to sin once for all, our 'risen' life here on earth is still under attack. It is true that God's Spirit already becomes here 'our spirit' (which Paul distinguishes sharply from the human mind—1 Cor. 14:14); but it happens in such a way that our spirit always needs the encouragement of the 'Spirit himself', of the Spirit of God always breaking through to it afresh (Rom. 8:15f.). The Holy Spirit is thus at one and the same time the one who calls and the one who answers within us. This life of God within our human life is then also the 'spirit' which, Paul anticipates, will pass through death and judgment and be saved (1 Cor. 5:5).

3. *John*

Here too the conversation with Nicodemus about birth from the Spirit ends with a reference to the Crucified (3:14f.), and the high priest who is obliged to prophesy in spite of himself speaks of him too (11:51f.). The reference however is not to the powerlessness of Jesus but to his 'lifting up', albeit the strange lifting up on the cross. But even this is God's victory (19:30). Whoever recognises this is 'born of the Spirit' (3:3, 6), from God, from above, from heaven, and no longer lives 'from the flesh', from below, from the earth, from this world, from the devil (3:6, 31; 8:23, 42-47; 15:19; 17:14, 16). But the Spirit is to be found in the words of Jesus which are 'spirit and life' (6:63; see 3:34). John is not therefore thinking of a spiritual world above, which we find when we leave the world of the flesh behind and go up to 'heaven', in spiritual experiences (see 3:13) or after death. John lays stress again upon what we have discovered from Paul: 'flesh' is actually anything other than Jesus. Thus the long metaphorical sayings of Jesus all make the same point: everything man seeks is to be found in him alone: 'the true light', 'the true bread', 'the true vine', 'the good shepherd' (1:9; 6:32; 15:1; 10:11). Whoever relies upon any other light, or bread, or vine, or shepherd, deceives himself. Only the Spirit, who flows from the Crucified (7:38, to be taken in this sense), can lead men into all the truth (16:13), to him who is *the* truth (14:6), as he recalls the community to him (14:26; 15:26).

The new creation begins at the point at which the Spirit 'begets' a man 'from above' (3:3)—which is how John interprets, in a new way, a traditional baptismal word (3:5; see Matt. 18:3). For him there is just one gift of the Spirit: the knowledge of Jesus. Therefore it is not by chance that he does not choose the metaphor of the body, in which one member has need of the other, but those of the flock, the ear of corn and the vine (10:1-18; 12:24; 15:1-6), where sheep side by side, grains of corn side by side, branches side by side, all live from the one, but do not have need of each other. I John 2:20, 27 gives a striking picture of a community in which all have knowledge and have need of no other teacher than the Spirit himself. All 'disciples' (whom John calls 'the twelve' only at 6:67) have received, along with the command to love one another as brothers, the power of the Holy Spirit to forgive sins (20:22f.). There is indeed a call to love (15:12-17; 1 John 3:14-18; 4:11-13, in what is perhaps a later addition); but it is love for the brotherhood, which specifically excludes love for the world (15:18-16:4; 1 John 2:15f.). It is true that the Spirit gives the power to witness and therewith responsibility for the world (15:26f.; 17:20-23); not however in such a way that the Christian community breaks out into the world and learns its language, as we find with Paul (1 Cor. 14:16, 23-25), but that, shielded from the world, it demonstrates by the way it lives what life under the leading of the Spirit means. In fact, in faith everything has already been attained. Of course this must be 'kept for eternal life', for the time when we fully behold God's glory (6:27; 12:25; 14:2f.; 17:24). But the decisive thing is not a man's conception of the world to come, but whether, through encountering Jesus, he already finds 'the resurrection and the life' (11:24f.). That is what the new birth from the Spirit is (3:5f.): through Jesus there bursts in a new life from a completely different dimension. The believer must die, it is true. But what the Spirit has begun to build in him will not be destroyed. Rather it will be brought to completion by God. To that extent he who believes in Jesus will not die, or if he dies will yet live (11:25f.).

4. WHERE THEN IS THE HOLY SPIRIT AT WORK?

The typical *'protestant' answer* is *not possible*: the working of the Holy Spirit cannot be 'frozen into' the written words of the Bible. He certainly speaks through Scripture (Mark 12:36; Heb. 10:15); but the antitheses of Matt. 5:21-48 show clearly how inadequately Scripture is understood when it is read literally. Paul can even declare (in spite of Rom. 3:21 etc.) that the Church should live 'not under the old written code but in the new life of the Spirit' (Rom. 7:6). In other words, if, with the help of Scripture, the Church tries to make herself secure, then Scripture is reduced to mere letters and law, and remains, along with its readers, under the 'veil'. It is the Spirit who first opens the heart and along with it the Scripture (2 Cor. 3:6, 14-18). According to John 3:1-10, even the most distinguished expositor of Scripture cannot understand Scripture (which bears witness to Jesus—John 5:39, 46f.) unless he is begotten again through the Spirit.

The typical *'catholic' answer* is *not possible.* Certainly the Spirit creates order. Ethical maxims and warnings of God's judgment come, we may presume, from prophets inspired by the Spirit and are attributed to the Spirit (Rev. 2:7, etc.). He also makes men 'guardians' (Acts 20:28), and gives to each his gift and his task, so that everything may proceed in an orderly fashion (1 Cor. 12:8-11; 14:32f.). In this, women play an important part (Acts 18:26; Rom. 16:1; 1 Cor. 11:5; Phil. 4:2f.; see John 4:39; 11:28; 20:18). The Spirit brings to mind what was taught 'from the beginning' (John 14:26; 1 John 2:7, 24). But it is *he* who calls men for particular forms of service; all the Church can do is give subsequent recognition to what he has already done (Acts 6:3; 20:28; 1 Cor. 12; 16:15-18; 1 Tim. 1:18; 4:14). Therefore the four Greek expressions for 'ministry' are used only for the work of Jewish or pagan officials, or for that of Christ or the whole community—never for that of an individual or group. What is basically said to Peter (and what constitutes his apostolic uniqueness—Matt. 16:18f.) applies to the whole community as his successor (Matt. 18:18). Even the special gift of a member of the community can at any time be given by the Spirit to another, in which case the first must sit down and let the other speak (1 Cor. 14:30). The leading of the Spirit is enough (1 John 2:27). Thus at the end of the New Testament period the pattern of the Pastoral Epistles, which speak of ordination (though only where the Spirit has pointed out through prophets the person to be ordained), stands alongside that of the Johannine Epistles, where the Spirit can speak through any member of the community (though only when this happens within the framework of what has been taught 'from the beginning'). Both forms are possible, so long as the provisos mentioned apply.

The purely *'charismatic' answer* is *not possible.* Even one of those who first received the Spirit at Pentecost, one called by Jesus himself, can be in error (Gal. 2:12). The most wonderful spiritual experiences can come from false gods (1 Cor. 12:2f.). Not every spirit comes from God and imparts the truth (1 John 4:1-6). Only their position in relation to the 'Lord' who 'has come in the flesh' shows what they are. But even prophecies clearly coming from the Spirit do not absolve a person from the need to make his own independent decision. The Spirit tells Paul not to go to Jerusalem (Acts 21:4), and yet that is exactly what he has to do, 'bound in the Spirit' (Acts 20:22). Even less can God's Spirit be guaranteed by indisputable miracles. It is not always as easy as in the case of the sons of Sceva, where 'the evil spirit' refuses the miracle (Acts 19:15f.; cf. Mk. 13:22; Acts 16:16; 2 Thess. 2:9; Rev. 13:13).

Does the Spirit then contradict himself? He installs bishops and imparts his charisma through ordination, yet at the same time teaches the Church that it has no need of teachers other than himself. He calls Paul to martyrdom, and at the same time warns him against it. He gives spiritual speech in overflowing measure, yet restrains the church member from using it freely in worship. Now we find that Jesus spoke in parables because God can never be taken over and manipulated, not even with the most correct formula; he must be able constantly to speak his Word afresh and lead us out towards new horizons. The Church spoke of the Spirit on the same basis. Of course there must be guidelines: the questions whether Jesus is acknowledged as truly man and heavenly Lord, and whether what is done leads to the building up of the Church as a whole. Of course, too, God is always giving to his Church people specially equipped to clarify these questions, and confessions of faith which try to safeguard the truth. We should be very grateful for that. But neither of these must ever stand in the way of the Spirit when he wants to speak afresh in a fresh situation. In face of the danger of a gnosis which threatens a general disintegration (1 Tim. 6:20) the Spirit can provide an ordered service of proclamation, and, equally, in face of the danger of a developing officialdom in the Church (3 John 9f.) he can remind the community of the absolute freedom of the Spirit. He can call a man to a task, and at the same time point out to him the hardness of the road he must travel. He can give overflowing joy and at the same time the sobriety of a love which never forgets others. He can speak in 'protestant', 'catholic' and 'charismatic' terms.

Translated by G. W. S. Knowles

Note

1. See 'Alles Nähere' in E. Schweizer *Heiliger Geist* (Kreuzverlag 1978).

Part I

Son and Spirit:
The Question of Orthodoxy

Dietrich Ritschl

The History of the
Filioque Controversy

IT IS MAINLY with reference to his action and presence that the Bible and Christians talk about the Holy Spirit. The 'filioque', on the other hand, is a concept drawn from the theology of the trinity. It is here that a particular difficulty arises for many people today. What are the connections between reflections on the trinity and the actual presence of the Spirit in our communities, in our own life? Perhaps this is a typically western question, but it must not be lost sight of in considering the 'filioque' controversy that since the later patristic period it has constituted an important reason for the split between the western and the Orthodox Churches.

1. *The filioque as a concept in the theology of the trinity*

In a lengthy process of theological development that was not in any way the result of deliberate intention, the Church of the west added to the creed of Nicaea and Constantinople (which is in fact the only genuinely ecumenical confession of faith) the word *filioque* in the statement about the Holy Spirit proceeding from the Father so that the clause now read *qui ex patre filioque procedit.* The thesis was that the Spirit has its origin from the Father *and* from the Son. It would be a complete misunderstanding of this addition if it were to be regarded as anything other than a theological statement about the inner relationships of the trinity. 'Within' the triune God, in the 'immanent trinity', the coming forth of the Spirit, his *processio,* is to be understood as a coming forth from the Father as well as from the Son. If one wants to understand the controversy about this *filioque* clause, then one has to think oneself back completely into the

3

type of argumentation used in classical trinitarian theology. In doing so one will discover that, contrary to one's immediate first impression, these ways of thought are extraordinarily relevant to our contemporary understanding of the Church, of ethics, of binding doctrine, and not least to how we judge the various charismastic movements that have sprung up recently. At a time when many of us hardly know how to provide theological justification for being able to talk about God at all, it may indeed seem rash to drag into the focus of our attention such a subtle question from the doctrine of the immanent trinity. But it is precisely by the study of this subtle question that it can be shown that western theology has all along had the tendency to encourage talk of God 'in general' and thus not concretely of the triune God. The modalistic tendency—the reduction as it were of Father, Son and Spirit to three aspects of the deity—in fact makes it difficult to talk of God.

2. The problem of the schism

Behind the controversy lies a difference in the way the doctrine of the trinity is conceived in the East and in the West. The central point of the controversy itself is the West's unilateral decision to add an important trinitarian clause to the universal profession of faith. For the oriental Churches this was unacceptable: (1) because it was an uncanonical addition, (2) because it was not in harmony with tradition, and (3) because it was dogmatically untrue and dangerous. This has been the basis of the noteworthy series of defences of the anti-filioque position which the Orthodox world has produced throughout the centuries from John of Damascus in the eighth century right up to Patriarch Anthimos's answer to Pope Leo XIII in 1894. Today the problem arises on two levels: (1) Does the filioque still continue to be rejected by the Orthodox Churches as something completely unacceptable and as a symptom of profound differences with regard to the Trinity and the Holy Spirit, or is it classified historically, and ultimately tolerated, as a typically Ambrosian and Augustinian peculiarity of western theology? But then: (2) What is the meaning of the fact that for the most part the Nicene creed does not in the west have the significance and dignity that are ascribed to it in the Orthodox world? As an addition to this creed the filioque does not in the west have all that great a significance—and it is here that there exists a surprising lack of symmetry between the Church's western and eastern wings. This must be taken into account not just in connection with the historical interpretation of the controversy but also and particularly in connection with the efforts that have recently begun to be made towards ending it.[1] Simply deleting the filioque from the creed would in the first place be no great sacrifice for most western Churches (some indeed are at the moment suggesting making this change), and in the second place—

and what is much more important—the theological question to which the filioque is the pointer would remain unanswered.

2. THE EXTERNAL HISTORICAL COURSE OF THE CONTROVERSY

The bare facts and data of the controversy yield remarkably little. This is surprising only to someone who is not aware that the filioque is merely the tip of an iceberg. It is nevertheless advisable to begin by listing the most important facts in order to run through them a second time and sketch in their theological background. Because many of the details cannot be mentioned here and at the same time there is no comprehensive modern account of the controversy, important historical studies and some theological works will have to be referred to in the notes.

It is particularly with regard to the filioque controversy[2] that in the west distinctions have to be drawn between theology and the Church and then within the Church between regional synods or councils and the Roman Church as a whole—and later of course between the latter and the non-Roman churches. From Tertullian (*Adversus Praxean*), Novatian (*de Trinitate*), Ambrose (*de Spiritu Sancto*), and above all Augustine (e.g., *de Trinitate, Epp.* 11 and 120, as well as his exegetical writings) onwards, western theology had in fact long advocated the filioque before it was accepted by individual councils or by the Church as a whole. While the filioque doctrine was expressed by the councils of Toledo[3] in 446-7 and 589 (the filioque clause found in the canons of the council of 400 is a later addition) and by those of Gentilly, Frankfurt, Friuli and Aachen, this does not mean that the western Church had taught this doctrine officially. It must further be noted that the later official filioque doctrine underwent a change in the grounds on which it was based and in the consequences drawn from it. Anselm and Thomas Aquinas to some extent adduce different reasons and draw different consequences in their teaching of the filioque from those adduced and drawn by the early Latin fathers.

Some general observations are also called for with regard to the churches of the east. Particularly with reference to Constantinople one must not forget the problems created by Latin missionary activity among the Slavs (especially the Bulgars) and above all the political strains in relations with Rome.[4] While it is only an indirect knowledge of the background of eastern Orthodox theology, especially trinitarian doctrine, that can be attributed to western theologians,[5] similarly there are good historical grounds for completely absolving eastern theologians and Church leaders of insight into the particular problems of the Church in Spain (the Arianism displayed by the Priscillianists) as well as of the

Frankish Church. It was precisely in these regions that the filioque clause first won acceptance. What this means is that major political problems and concerns as well as the lack of information both about Church politics and about theology played their part from the beginning in determining the shape of the controversy. If one thinks of the outcome of the attempts at reunion of the councils of Lyons (1274) and Florence (1439) one must conclude by judging that the possibilities for understanding plainly diminished with the centuries.

(a) The most essential external facts of the controversy are the following. As early as the early fifth century the filioque clause was in liturgical use in Spain: it appears in the canons of the council of Toledo of 446-7 and also in the Athanasian creed[6] (*Spiritus sanctus a Patre et Filio ... procedens,* DS 75, section 23), as well as in the third and fourth councils of Toledo (589 and 633) and in the councils of Gentilly (767) and Frankfurt (794). At the council of Friuli (796) the filioque was defended by Paulinus of Aquileia. But before the middle of the eighth century there had come the first weightier clarification on the eastern side from the pen of John of Damascus (*Expos. fid. orth.* I:8:12), a treatment which would continually be referred back to later.

(b) The occasion for Leo III's questioning Charlemagne on the subject was the harassing of Frankish monks of the monastery of St Sabas in Jerusalem on account of the introduction of the filioque into the liturgy. The emperor in 809 asked Theodulf of Orleans to provide a theological treatment of the question,[7] and at the synod of Aachen the disputed formula was introduced into the creed. Due for frequent citation afterwards was the pope's attitude of reserve: the filioque clause was indeed stated to be orthodox at the synod of Rome in 810, but its introduction into the creed was rejected. (It was on this occasion that the two silver tablets were engraved with the unamended text of the creed and put on public display.)

One would not therefore go astray if one were to see the Frankish Church, the court of Charlemagne (with Alcuin's *De processione Spiritus sancti*), and the earlier difficulties in Spain as the context in which Augustine's theological concept became a constituent part of the creed that was accepted in terms of the Church's life, worship and canon law.

(c) The starting-point of the controversy proper, however, is Photius, who in 858 displaced Ignatius as patriarch of Constantinople. The following juxtaposition of events in west and east may perhaps illustrate the prevailing confusion:

863 Pope Nicholas I confirms the deposed Ignatius in his office.	The emperor Michael III appeals to the Pope in Rome.

The Latin Church lays claim to Bulgaria.	867 Photius condemns the Latin mission in Bulgaria and the filioque. A council in Constantinople excommunicates Pope Nicholas; but with the accession of Basil as emperor Ignatius is reinstated.
869 Rome condemns Photius.	869 Constantinople confirms the condemnation.
870 Rome condemns Ignatius' claim to Bulgaria.	877 Ignatius dies, Photius becomes patriarch again.
880 Papal legates in Constantinople subscribe to the creed without the filioque clause and confirm Photius' reinstatement (thus F. Dvornik as against earlier research).	879-80 Council of Constantinople revokes the decision of 869.
	886 The emperor Leo VI deposes Photius.
892 Rome excommunicates Photius (Dvornik regards this as a later legend).[8]	cf. Photius' *Liber de Spiritus sancti mystagogia* (Migne PG 102).

(*d*) The next stage of the controversy is just as much marked by political pressures and confusion as is the preceding one. In 1009 Pope Sergius IV used the filioque in a letter to Constantinople summarising the faith; his namesake in that city (deliberately?) omitted the name of the pope of Rome from the diptychs. Five years later Pope Benedict VIII, who was certainly more interested in wars against Saracens and Greeks than in theology, responded to pressure from the emperor Henry II and officially and finally included the filioque in what thus became the western form of the Nicene creed. It was now sung at Mass.

(*e*) Still to be mentioned before the fall of Byzantium on May 29 1453, when Orthodox and Latins celebrated the eucharist together in Hagia Sophia before the end came, are the reunion councils of Lyons (1274) and Florence (1438-39) with the humiliations these entailed for the Orthodox world. As is well known, the Orthodox delegates at Lyons were not able to make their support for the filioque prevail in their own churches on their return, while after Florence there was no announcement of the council's results in the east. The real theological dispute had become deplorably reduced to the bickerings and wranglings of ecclesiastical politics, and in these terms no solution was possible. Political intrigue, confused struggling for power and genuine theological learning had become too tangled up with each other in the person of Photius—for whom the west could offer no theological counterpart of equal standing—to enable the theological problem of the internal relations of the trinity to be seen as clearly as it had been by classical Greek and later Augustinian theology in their first efforts to think the question through. The medieval theologians of the west, especially Anselm and Thomas, combined other concerns with the long-standing question. Their ideas moved yet further away from a possible consensus with the east.

(f) Finally, a variety of attitudes was shown by the non-Roman churches of the west. For centuries the filioque clause was no longer the subject of ecclesiastical political or legal wrangles. It was not dealt with in the few scanty contacts between the Reformed and Orthodox Churches. Because of the high value they placed on the Athanasian creed, the Reformers and both the Lutheran and the Reformed confessions of faith stayed loyal to the filioque clause. But the controversy was not renewed by Cyril Lucaris, the Greek theologian and patriarch with Calvinist leanings who was murdered in 1638, while a little later the influential Peter Mogila, who knew the west just as well and who introduced Latin into the academic world of Kiev and far beyond, once again made rejection of the papal primacy and of the filioque a central point in his *Orthodox Confession* (1642-3). The softening of the western attitude, as shown by Pope Benedict XIV, who did not want to maintain the filioque as a condition for a union with the eastern Church,[9] did not have any effect. By contrast Leo XIII's invitation to reunion of 1894 provoked a stern reply from Patriarch Anthimos, who accused the western Church of arrogant innovations and of placing obstacles in the way of reunion, with explicit reference to the filioque, papal infallibility, the doctrine of purgatory, the use of unleavened bread in the eucharist, etc. If the pope could show that these doctrines had been the joint inheritance of east and west before the ninth century, then a reunion was possible. This brought an argument based on tradition to the centre of the stage.

(g) More complex are the relations between the Orthodox world and the Anglican Communion[10] and of course between it and the Old Catholic Church, which in 1875 deleted the filioque clause from the Nicene creed.[11] After originally defending the filioque (Roger Hutchinson), Anglican theologians as early as the seventeenth century (John Pearson, Edward Stillingfleet) began to interpret and analyse the theological conception of the filioque, a process that only really got going after 1833 in the train of the Oxford movement. As Pearson had already done, a distinction was rightly drawn between the 'eternal procession' of the Spirit and his 'temporal mission', but there was no question yet of a rejection of the filioque clause, althouth one of the leading participants in the discussion, the well-known scholar and hymn-writer J. M. Neale, was inclined to reject the filioque completely. At the Bonn Conferences with the Orthodox and the Old Catholics in 1874 and 1875, on the other hand, the English representative E. B. Pusey defended the western view of the filioque. The Joint Doctrinal Commission of 1931 repeated the consensus reached in 1875, that John of Damascus's formula 'through the Son' (instead of 'and from the Son') was useful with regard to a possible reunion. But real progress had to wait till the meeting of this commission held in Moscow in 1976. The filioque was then rejected by the Anglican delegation as part of the universal creed because: (1) the sentence in the creed about the Spirit proceeding from the Father was concerned with the Spirit's eternal *processio,* not his historical *missio*; (2) the addition of the filioque clause to the creed did not rest on universal agreement; and finally (3) the creed constituted the public confession of faith by the people of God in the eucharist.[12] The 1978 Lambeth Conference endorsed this Moscow agreed statement and asked member churches of the Anglican Communion to consider omitting the filioque from the Nicene creed.[13]

3. THE COURSE OF THE INNER THEOLOGICAL CONTROVERSY

With the decision of the Old Catholic Church and the recommendations of the Anglican Communion, this survey of the most important historical events in the development of the filioque dispute has concluded by leading us back to the centre of the problem—to the question rooted in the internal relationships of the trinity, of how we understand the Spirit's origin from the Father. Here in fact theological developments in the Augustinian tradition of the west followed quite different paths from those taken by the Greek theology of the east. The aim of the following is to provide a brief sketch of all this.

1. *Athanasius's conceptual legacy*

What is of the greatest importance is the way in which Greek theological reflection is embedded in the doxological language of the liturgy. Theological concepts are meant to be an aid to genuine worship. This is already quite clear in the case of the classical architect of trinitarian doctrine, Athanasius.[14] In any event in his writings the distinctions between important terms like *ousia* (Latin *substantia,* substance, essence), *hypostasis,* and *prosopon* (Latin *persona*), as well as *physis* and *energeia,* are not as clear and unequivocal as people liked to think later when referring to his work. The west, too, relied on Athanasius. But his real heirs are the three great Cappadocians, Basil, Gregory of Nazianzus and Gregory of Nyssa, and it was only with them that, apart from exceptions, the use of concepts became clear. What was it all about?

Although one cannot separate the 'energies' in God from his *ousia*, it is impossible for the believer with his or her knowledge to penetrate as it were directly to God's *ousia*. Just as everything in creation has its being in the divine 'energies', so too does the believer in his or her participation in the triune God. This insight, which in essence is already to be found in Athanasius, who was thereby able to link creation and redemption, underwent a long development to reach its fully elaborated form in the theology of Gregory Palamas (who died in 1358), in whose work the uncreated 'energies' of the trinity are seen in their relationship with the experience of belief. But in his polemical writings *Contra Arianos* and in his friendly letters of clarification *Ad Serapionem* Athanasius had already been teaching that Father, Son and Spirit rest in each other (Irenaeus had already said this of the Father and the Son), that we must think no less of the Spirit than of the second person of the trinity, and above all that the believer's participation in God is itself a sharing in the Holy Spirit. But because this is a union with God *through the Son,* through the *Word,* it is through and because of Jesus Christ that believers are sharers in God in the Spirit. It is in this sense that we are meant to understand the constantly repeated formula *dia tou hyiou* ('through the Son') that is later to become a matter of dispute. Athanasius says the Father is 'above everything' and also 'through everything and in everything', the Son 'through everything' and the Spirit 'in all things' (or 'everything'). Communion with God is thus with the Father, who is always Father of the Son, in the Spirit. The Spirit shares so completely and integrally in the Father and in the *Logos,* and this on account of the complete unity of God's activities and being (of his *energeia*), that it can also be asked whether the later interpretation has not read into Athanasius too sharp a division between God's *ousia* and his *energeia*. It is in any case clear that at all levels of his argument Athanasius is not just talking about God as he is in himself (the 'immanent trinity') but talking about him as he is *ad extra,* to the believers who acknowledge and praise him. Athanasius could thus be interpreted as allowing a shift from the order of knowledge ('in the Spirit, through the Son, from the Father') to the internal ordering (*taxis*) of the trinity.

2. *Clarifying the concepts—the Cappadocians*

The Cappadocians do not in any way neglect the soteriological dimension of Athanasius's doctrine of the trinity—its relationship in other words to the effecting of salvation and mankind's share in this. But they deepen and differentiate the doctrine of God's triune being. Basil provides a more careful definition of *hypostasis* but is still vague when it comes to expressing himself about the Spirit's origin from the Father. Gregory of Nazianzus supplemented this by providing a meaning for the newfound concept of the Spirit's *ekporeusis,* his coming forth, while the youngest of the three, Gregory of Nyssa, investigated the concept *dia tou hyiou* ('through the Son'). All three are unanimous in being concerned that the Holy Spirit should not be misunderstood as something 'created' (*ktisma*). Basil, who is inclined to distinguish between the inner ordering (*taxis*) of the three persons and their external appearance, is concerned to avoid any confusion between the characteristics (*prosopon* could be thus translated) of the Son and of the Spirit. The Son's quality of being begotten does not apply to the Spirit. Gregory of Nazianzus continues by teaching that the distinguishing quality of the Spirit is his *ekporeusis,* parallel to the Son's *gennesia* (being begotten). This parallelism is an important point for understanding the orthodox doctrine of the trinity: while Athanasius and even Basil could in certain circumstances be interpreted as implying Father, Son and Spirit being ranged alongside one another, such a view is from now on prevented. The younger Gregory teaches conclusively that God, the life-giving force, is the only source (*pege*), root (*rhiza*), principle (*arche*) and cause (*aitia*). While one can therefore say the Father's Spirit comes to the faithful 'through the Son', such a statement is meaningless, not to say misleading, in the context of the trinity's inner dynamics, because it suggests the idea that in the deity there are two sources, two causes, two roots. The Orthodox teaching now becomes that the Father is the unique source of Son and Spirit, because this is his hypostatic distinguishing quality, to bring forth the Son and the Spirit; these in their turn have their hypostases that cannot be interchanged. The concept is thus dominated by the Father's *monarchia.* The western *filioque* cannot of course be reconciled with this view.

The question does admittedly arise whether Orthodox theology with its Aristotelian categories of cause and hypostasis can provide a satisfactory answer to the question which cropped up in the west. How in his eternal *ekporeusis* is the Spirit linked with the Son? Is not the Father breathing out the Spirit already the Father of the Son? Two dangers do not seem to be avoided: (1) that the Father is placed above the other two hypostases thanks to his own hypostatic function; and (2) that the Holy Spirit is not unequivocally the 'Spirit of Christ' as one nevertheless always wants to call him, following the New Testament, with reference to the trinity seen not as immanent but as reflecting the economy of salvation.

3. *Augustine and the western tradition of thought*

What is well known and can only be alluded to here is the persistent influence exerted on the western tradition by Augustine's understanding of the *relationes* in the trinity. In this the distinctive qualities of the three *personae* (now, following Tertullian, the western concept) disappear more and more. Harnack may have exaggerated when he took the view that Augustine would 'himself never have arrived at the trinity if he had not been tied to tradition'.[15] But the west certainly has the triangular construction of Augustine's modalistic view to thank for the tendency towards a merely monotheistic idea of God. His reflection did not, like that of the Greeks, start with the Father but with the abstract idea of trinity as such, whereby the three persons mutually limit and condition each other in symmetrical *relationes*—to such an extent that he teaches the Son's participation in his own mission. It is ultimately only reference to the Bible that prevents the logically possible idea that the Father or even the Son proceeds from the Spirit. *Processio* is thus used in a much broader sense than is permitted by the Greek definitions of the uninterchangeable hypostatic qualities. This becomes clear in Anselm (*De processione Spiritus sancti*) and in later scholastic theology.

4. *The ecumenical task*

If Orthodox theologians point to the fact[16] that the western doctrine of the trinity makes impossible the spiritual transfiguration of the believer in a participation in the Father in the Spirit, western theology can counter with the criticism that the operation of the Spirit does not in the Orthodox doctrine of the trinity appear clearly enough as co-ordinated with the entire work of Christ. To express this is the real concern of the filioque, and in our century it has once again been advocated as strongly as possible by Karl Barth.[17] However, the most recent developments indicate that the example of the Old Catholic and Anglican Churches will exert an influence on the remainder of the western churches in the direction of self-criticism of the un-trinitarian (or only intellectually trinitarian) concept of God in the Augustinian tradition.[18] At the same time what is awaited from Orthodox theology is some help towards a clarification of the Spirit's relation to the Son. What in one context means the danger of mere monotheism together with a trinitarian tradition that is not understood by the people becomes in the other the construction of a monopatrism which is expressed in the general concepts of Greek theology and which allows the persistence of the ecclesiological and ethical dimension of the 'Spirit of Christ' in the liturgical language of praise.

The core of the question can only be expressed in theological, not historical, terms. What form should be adopted today by a doctrine of the trinity that we can really cope with? The models available up till now are understandable, up to and including the dilemmas they contain, but can they be used?

Translated by Robert Nowell

Notes

1. See the discussions at the 1978 Lambeth Conference as well as the draft resolutions for the General Assembly of the Church of Scotland, May 1979. A study group of the Faith and Order Commission on the filioque question met in October 1978 and has circulated a memorandum which will be the subject of further discussion and revision this year.

2. See H. B. Swete's classic monograph *On the History of the Doctrine of the Procession of the Holy Spirit from the Apostolic Age to the Death of Charlemange* (Cambridge 1876); M. Jugie 'Origine de la controverse sur l'addition du Filioque au symbole' *Revue des Sciences Philosophiques et Théologiques* 28 (1939) pp. 369ff.; and also F. Dvornik *The Photian Schism: History and Legend* (Cambridge 1948).

3. The canons of the various councils of Toledo are to be found in Migne PL 84, cols. 327-562: they reflect the Spanish Church's special problems during this period.

4. Cf. F. Dvornik *Byzance et la Primauté Romaine* (Paris 1964).

5. Many years of research into the reception of eastern theology are summarised by B. Altaner *Revue Bénédictine* 62 (1952) pp. 201ff.

6. On its contents and date see J. N. D. Kelly *The Athanasian Creed* (London/New York 1964).

7. *De processione Spiritus sancti* Migne PL 105, cols. 187ff.

8. In addition to Dvornik see the earlier article by F. Kattenbusch, 'Photius' *Realencyclopädie* (Stuttgart ³1904 pp. 374-93).

9. In 1742. But cf. the *Professio fidei Orientalibus (Maronitis) praescripta of 1743*, DS 2525-2540.

10. See the contributions to H. M. Waddams (ed.) *Anglo-Russian Theological Conference* (London 1958) as well as H. A. Hodges *Anglicanism and Orthodoxy* (London 1955), and the articles by N. Zernov and G. Florovsky in R. Rouse and S. C. Neill (edd.) *A History of the Ecumenical Movement* (London 1954).

11. See S. Zankov 'Beziehungen zwischen Alt-Katholiken und Orthodoxe Kirchen' *Internationale kirchliche Zeitschrift* 52 (1962) pp. 26ff.

12. K. Ware and C. Davey (edd.) *Anglican-Orthodox Dialogue: The Moscow Statement Agreed by the Anglican-Orthodox Joint Doctrinal Commission 1976* (London 1977) pp. 87-88.

13. *The Report of the Lambeth Conference 1978* (London 1978) pp. 51-52.

14. See D. Ritschl *Athanasius* (Zürich 1964); T. F. Torrance 'Athanasius: A study in the foundations of classical theology' in *Theology in Reconciliation* (London 1975) pp. 215-266; and T. C. Campbell 'The doctrine of the Holy Spirit in . . . Athanasius' *Scottish Journal of Theology* 4 (1974) pp. 408-440.

15. A. von Harnack *Dogmengeschichte (Grundriss)* (Tübingen 1931) p. 237.

16. For example, V. Lossky *The Mystical Theology of the Eastern Church* (London 1957) and *The Vision of God* (London/Clayton, Wisconsin 1963).

17. K. Barth *Church Dogmatics* I:1 (Edinburgh 1936) pp. 533-560. For a critique cf. G. S. Hendry *The Holy Spirit in Christian Theology* (London 1965) pp. 45ff., and for an alternative proposal A. I. C. Heron 'Who proceedeth from the Father and the Son' *Scottish Journal of Theology* 4 (1971) pp. 149-166, and D. L.

Berry 'Filioque and the Church' *Journal of Ecumenical Studies* vol. 5 No. 3 (1968) pp. 535-554.

18. See on the effect of Augustine D. Ritschl *Konzepte I, Gesammelte Aufsätze, Patristische Studien* (Berne 1976) pp. 102-140.

Michael Fahey

Son and Spirit: Divergent Theologies between Constantinople and the West

THE LONG-STANDING debates about the *Filioque* between Byzantium and the West which continue even in our day could lead to the mistaken opinion that in fact the two churches do not share common views about the Holy Spirit. Actually both Latin and Greek speaking Christians shared the same faith as do East and West today about the Spirit's inspiration of Holy Scripture, about the Spirit's presence in the sacraments of the Church, in charisms and graces poured out by the Spirit upon believers. In both churches the Spirit of God is seen as guiding saints and helping bishops gathered at local synods and ecumenical councils. Reading ancient liturgical texts, one would be hard put, apart from the different languages, to identify this liturgy as typically Eastern and that one Western, in regard to its view of the Spirit. The idea that somehow the West is exclusively Christomonist in its faith and practice is a flight of fancy.

1. A LATE CONTROVERSY

As far as functional or 'economical' pneumatology is concerned, there exists a shared faith even to our day. But the churches have long differed on the choice of language to describe the Spirit within the internal life of the Blessed Trinity. Perhaps in retrospect both churches have been overly ambitious in attempting to do what may well be impossible. Still their

15

attempts were never intended as an exercise in idle speculation, but as a careful preservation of the ancient traditions under attack. Both the Old and New Rome reacted with common distrust against heresies related to the Holy Spirit that developed in the Church, rather late, at least by comparison to the earlier Christological controversies. Both East and West opposed Montanism, with its weird teaching that the Paraclete had become incarnate; they opposed with equal vigour the Pneumatomachians and other heretical teachers. Not before the seventh century was there an awareness that liturgical and theological terms used to describe the interior life of the Blessed Trinity, especially in regard to the 'procession' of the Holy Spirit, were different.

1. An 'East-West' Conflict?

As is clear from the article reviewing the history of the *Filioque* controversy, this divergence between Byzantium and Rome was part of a far broader estrangement of long duration. Strictly speaking, the controversy is not between East and West. Rather than grouping several distinctive Church traditions under the rubric 'Eastern', it is proper to be more restrictive and speak of 'Byzantine' theologies connected with the Patriarchate of Constantinople. Other Eastern traditions such as the Syrian, Egyptian and Armenian, were not directly involved in the *Filioque* question. The tension developed between the Old Rome and the New Rome (Constantinople) or perhaps more accurately between Constantinople and Aachen, symbol of the growing Frankish influence in the Latin Church especially after the establishment under Charlemagne of a Holy 'Roman' Empire. Constantinople saw this new empire as divisive, thwarting the ancient 'Roman' dream of ecumenical and political unity. Had the Latin and Greek theological writings from the two centres of the Mediterranean world been better known, had the different churches keener sympathies for the pastoral challenges facing various churches, much of the bitter controversy might have been avoided.

2. A Legitimate Variant in the Fight against Arianism?

Several ironies marked the development of different credal explanations about the procession of the Holy Spirit. The Frankish West, especially at the early local councils that took place in Toledo (A.D. 589, 633) relied on a creed they mistakenly, with the rest of the Latin Church through the Middle Ages, attributed to St Athanasius, the so-called Athanasian Creed or *Quicunque*.[1] It is only in our day that we know that the creed was actually written first in Latin about A.D.500 in Southern Gaul, a text cited early by Caesarius of Arles (d. 542). This creed, which mentioned a procession of the Holy Spirit from the Father and the Son, was congenial to the council fathers at Toledo because it served to present a markedly anti-Arian Christology. For if the Spirit proceeded from both the Father and Son, then the Son was not in any way inferior to the Father, as the Arian position implied. So when Visigoth King Reccared I entered the Catholic Church from Arianism (A.D. 589), it was useful to have a credal statement that was unabashedly anti-Arian. The West was not tinkering with pneumatology but asserting a strong Christological faith.

When the Byzantine Church later realised that there was a different Western formula, it saw this as one further exemplification of Frankish pretensions, proof of Roman fears before Frankish rulers, and ultimately Roman capitulation to Frankish demands to insert the *Filioque* into the sacrosanct Nicene creed. When the East became aware of the different credal formulation 'and from the Son' in Pope Martin I's synodal letter to Constantinople (649), it was a Byzantine monk, St Maximus the Confessor, who defended the different formula simply as a variation, quite legitimate, for the Byzantine form. He wrote: '[The Latins wished] to show he comes forth through him and to expose the connection and immutability of the substance' (PG 91:136).

The Greek Church maintained an intimate relationship between the Holy Spirit and Jesus Christ the Son of God. On the level of *mission* the Spirit was seen as being sent into the world by the Son. But Byzantine theology stayed close to the New Testament formulas, although in the earlier anti-Arian controversy at the Council of Nicaea the East had not been afraid of using the non-Scriptural word *homoousios* to assert that the Son is one in substance with the Father. The Byzantine tradition generally remained close to the language of the New Testament, especially John's Gospel. The word '*procession*' was rooted in Jesus' statement at the Last Supper that the Paraclete 'proceeds from the Father' (John 15:25). Constantinople had a variety of expressions for describing the relationship of Spirit and Son, but the favourite was one that appeared in the Gospel of St John, that the Spirit 'receives' from the Son (See John 16:14).

The formulation about the procession of the Spirit from both the Father and the Son, *ab utroque,* appears in the Western tradition during the last third of the fourth century. In various ways it is found in the works of Ambrose, Victorinus, Rufinus and others. Hilary of Poitiers had prepared the way for St Augustine by developing Tertullian's notion that the procession of the Spirit is effected through the Son. However modern scholars are less confident in citing these early texts that were once collected into florilegia of proof-texts about the Spirit's procession from Father and Son. It is not that certain that the citations were addressing the internal structure or nature of the Blessed Trinity and not simply what we would call today the temporal *ad extra* missions of the Spirit.

2. AUGUSTINE'S INFLUENCE IN THE WEST

St Augustine of Hippo did not create the doctrine of the procession from the Father and Son. However, the West was to draw upon Augustine's comments on the Spirit's procession *ab utroque* as he expressed them in the treatise *On the Trinity,* especially Chapter 15, which he completed about A.D. 416. His writings gave subsequent justification for the choice of that formula, although he himself had not been involved in the construction of the *Quicunque* creed, nor had he conceived of adding to the Nicene Creed. Had the East been able to read Augustine's entire Latin treatise, and for that matter if more Westerners made use of it more responsibly, it is doubtful that there would have arisen such antipathy for Augustinian trinitarian theology which lasts even today in the East, although his theology actually has similarities with Greek treatises on the Holy Spirit. Those who dismiss his work as abstract or purely philosophical simply betray that they have not read his major work on the Trinity.

1. *Towards an Authentic Understanding of Augustine's position*

Latin theology following Augustine came to argue that on the level of origin, the generation of the Son precedes the procession of the Holy Spirit. The Son in being generated by the Father receives from him all his perfections and all attributes, with the single exception of his paternity. The Son therefore receives from the Father his divine nature and with it that which spirates the Holy Spirit. Consequently, the Father in union with the Son is the principle of the Holy Spirit's procession.

What Byzantine theology has not always appreciated is that the Latins, including Augustine, perceived the Father as the special source or origin, the *origo principalis,* within the Trinity. The Holy Spirit proceeds from the Father, said Augustine, *principaliter*; he proceeds from the Father and Son *communiter* because of the gift that the Father makes to the Son. For the East the Father is the *principium sine principio* and it would have been difficult for the East to think of a *principium de principio.* Byzantine theologians were hesitant to associate the Son in the procession of the Spirit from the Father, because this appeared as a double procession. Terms such as *principium, causa, auctor,* even *procedere,* when converted to Greek equivalents, did not always convey the same meaning. This was especially true when Byzantine theologians tried to preserve the basic 'monarchy' of God the Father, the primordial *archē* of the divinity.

But when the West said that the Spirit proceeds from the Father and the Son, this did not mean that the Father was prevented from being the source or *archē* of the whole of divinity. Nor did it mean that the Spirit proceeds from the Son independently of the Father, nor that there are two spirations or two principles. The fact that this has been misunderstood is seen by the need at the Council of Florence in its declaration *Laetentur caeli* of July 6 1439, to insist that the Spirit's procession was '*ab uno principio et unica spiratione*' (DS 1300), a text used even earlier at the unsuccessful reunion council of Lyons II in 1274 (see DS 850).

Trinitarian theology—called rather by Greek theologians 'triadology'—can only be a search for partial understanding of an article of faith hidden in mystery. It is an attempt to express the idea of the unity and diversity, the three hypostases or persons in God. Triadology tries to express how in God there can be simultaneously a monad and triad, one and three. Byzantine theology complains that the common divine essence is not the principle of unity in the three persons. Rather it is the Father who is the unique source of the divine hypostases of the Son and the Spirit; the Father as person determines their origins and communicates to them his essence. To them the Father is *anarchos,* without a principle, and for the East the relationship of origin could not be the basis of the hypostases. Hence the reluctance of Constantinople to accept the West's system which it saw as based on the opposition of relationships. Latin theology, it was felt, disturbs the subtle balance between the absolute unity of the essence and the absolute diversity of the three persons. The West's trinitarian theology seemed to have introduced a dyadic conception of the Trinity. The divine essence or *ousia* seems to be distorted into an abstract idea of divinity, a rational essence binding the three divine individuals as, say, humanity might bind together men.

2. *An Orthodox Proposal for the Resolution of the Conflict*

One modern Orthodox proposal intended to eliminate much of the conflict that has been occasioned by the *Filioque* is that offered by the Greek theologian John Romanides.[2] Basically his reasoning is that there never was a *Filioque* controversy between the West and East Romans, only a conflict between all the Romans in the East and West versus the Franks. The 'Roman' position, that of the Old and New Rome, about the *Filioque* remained the same until the Western Romans capitulated to the Frankish power. Thus the *Filioque* controversy should be seen as essentially a continuation of Frankish efforts to control the whole Roman world.

Romanides further argues that the differences between Ambrose and Augustine are a summary of the differences between Roman and Frankish theological method and doctrine. He states that the worst mistake of the Frankish Church was to draw so uncritically and exclusively upon the theology of one theologian, Augustine, who was at best a confused and muddled thinker, one misguided by extraneous philosophies. According to this opinion, Augustine transformed the doctrine of the Trinity into a speculative exercise, thereby destroying the simplicity and biblical nature of the doctrine in the common Roman teaching, and adversely influencing the subsequent Western scholastic tradition.

Romanides' suggestion has a certain appeal because it sounds so simple. But unfortunately it is based on serious misunderstandings of the real character of Augustine's writings and schematises what was actually a much more complex development in the West. While it is true that cultural and political forces were at play in the subsequent defence of the *Filioque,* there were far more religious and pastoral reasons that led to the development of another theological tradition. There is little advantage in trying to heal the wounds of the *Filioque* controversy by distorting the reasons for its appearance, misunderstanding the dangers of 'Filioquism' and laying the blame at the feet of a presumably muddled theologian named Augustine of Hippo. Life is never that simple, nor is theological development.

3. THE EASTERN OBJECTIONS TO ADDITIONS TO THE CREED

1. *Interpretation or Innovation?*

The debate over the addition of the *Filioque* is also connected with the legitimacy of adding to the Nicene Creed.[3] The Third Ecumenical Council of the undivided Church held at Ephesus in A.D. 431 had stated: 'The holy synod enacted that it was lawful for no one to put forward, that is to write or compose, *another faith* than that defined by the holy Fathers congregated in the Holy Spirit at Nicaea' (DS 265). The West did not interpret this prohibition to include adding clarifications or in answering erroneous conceptions by inserting other words. The West reasoned that since the Church is a living society it can never renounce its mission to preserve intact the treasury of divine revelation. So that if it decided that it was pastorally expedient to add some words that did not distort the faith, indeed words that preserved the true faith, then this was not innovating but simply continuing a process begun at earlier councils. It is true that this reasoning remained at first implicit and became the subject of explicit reflection only after Byzantine objections to the addition of *Filioque.*

One of the clearest explanations of why the West felt justified in adding a word was given at the Council of Florence in the fifteenth century. The Western theologians explained that the *Filioque* was added because 'the *Filioque* as an explanation of those words [i.e., of the Nicene Creed] was legitimately and reasonably joined to the creed to declare its truth, since there was an urgent necessity at that time' (DS 1302). That clarification was acceptable to the Greeks who were present at Florence and who had participated in the long debates on the controverted issue. It is true that the *Filioque* did not begin with an ecumencial council, but when it was first added it was not intended to be imposed upon all churches. In its later history, of course, the West has tried to impose that addition on other churches even at times on Eastern churches in full communion with Rome.

2. *The Influence of Photius*

Photius, Patriarch of Constantinople from 858-867 and again from 878-886, played an enormous role in the subsequent debate between Byzantine and western theologians on the *Filioque* question.[4] It is interesting to speculate whether the strong feelings that the *Filioque* still generates in the East would be as pronounced if Photius had not taken such a vehement position in the ninth century. Many of the arguments that are still read in Greek theology are traceable to Photius' encyclical to the eastern Patriarchs of A.D. 866 where he states that the *Filioque* destroys the monarchy of the Father and relativises the reality of the personal or hypostatic existence of the Trinity. For Photius the *Filioque* was the 'crown of evils', product of a poorly educated West.

At the same time Photius himself introduced an element that seems in the judgment of many scholars not only in the West to be innovative. For Photius stated that the true patristic principle about the Holy Spirit is that the Spirit proceeds from the *Father alone* (ek *monou* Patros ekporeuetai). Was Photius going beyond the Patristic tradition to state on the basis of silence in the Johannine Gospel and in many Greek Fathers that the Spirit's procession was meant to be from the Father and from the Father alone? Even Russian theologians such as Bulgakov would argue that Photius misunderstood the Patristic position. Other statements of Photius in his famous *Mystagogy Concerning the Doctrine of the Holy Spirit* seemed clearly to go beyond the evidence at hand, as for instance his claim that the procession of the Holy Spirit from the Son is a heretical position anathematised by seven ecumenical councils (PG 102, 285).

The West has long needed a rehabilitation of Photius as a churchman and saint. Much of what is attributed to Photius' motives and intentions are simply products of polemical western writings. But this much-needed rehabilitation does not require us to hold that he understood Augustine, the Augustinian tradition, the pastoral problems of the Frankish Church, or indeed what the patristic period prior to him had actually said about the Spirit's procession from the *Father alone*.

3. *Towards the Future*

The riches of historical and patristic studies now offer the churches of East and West further insights into the reasons for different developments in the first millennium of Christianity. With these historical tools available to the churches and with a renewed spirit of love between the churches of the Old and New Rome, exemplified in the reconciliation between Paul VI and Athenagoras I, it is now possible to move to a new stage in fraternal understanding. What will have to disappear is the all too facile categorisations or denigrations of theologies that differ in emphasis but not in orthodoxy.[5] It will not help the re-establishment of full communion between East and West to form caricatures of theologies: The West's is philosophic, the East's is mystical, one is kataphatic, the other apophatic, one is liturgical, the other juridical. These sorts of assessments that are still found in manuals of theology simply perpetuate the appalling ignorance of one another's traditions. These traditions are never fully understood by identifying them with one theologian, be he Augustine, Thomas Aquinas, Gregory Palamas, or whoever.

Today it is not enough for Catholicism to deal with the Patriarchate of Constantinople, nor indeed with all the Orthodox churches. Rome must have as its partner all the major churches of the West, and the East must include the churches of the Ancient Oriental traditions antedating the Council of Chalcedon. Whether the decision reached in prayer is to drop the *Filioque* or to retain it in some churches, what is important is a deeper comprehension of workings of the Holy Spirit in different ages, and different traditions. Not to appreciate the truth expressed in other traditions is to be blind to the saving grace of the Spirit of God.

Notes

1. J. N. D. Kelly *The Athanasian Creed* (New York 1964).

2. J. Romanides 'The Filioque' in *Kleronomia* 7 (1975) pp. 285-314.

3. H. J. Marx *Filioque und Verbot eines anderen Glaubens auf dem Florentinum* (St Augustin 1977).

4. R. Haugh *Photius and the Carolingians. The Trinitarian Controversy* (Belmont, Mass. 1975), especially pp. 159-177. See also J. Pelikan *The Spirit of Eastern Christendom (600-1700)* (The Christian Tradition 2) (Chicago 1974), especially pp. 183-198.

5. T. O'Connor 'Homoousios and Filioque: An ecumenical analogy' in *Downside Review* 83 (1965) 1-19; and D. L. Berry 'Filioque and the Church' *Journ. Ecum. Stud.* 5 (1968) pp. 535-554.

Theodore Stylianopoulos

The Orthodox Position

THE ORTHODOX position on the Filioque has traditionally been uncompromising: the Filioque is nothing less than a scandal both as an arbitrary addition to the (Nicene) Creed against the supreme authority of the Ecumenical Councils as well as a theological error of grave implications. Peter of Antioch, an Orthodox bishop of the eleventh century, described it as a 'wicked thing, and among the wicked things the most wicked'. Contemporary Orthodox theologians still view the Filioque as a major issue of division between eastern and western Christians, second only to that of the primacy of the pope (in its absolute form). Some would see the Filioque as the foremost issue of division because, they contend, the Filioque is the source of all subsequent errors of western theology, including the teaching about absolute papal primacy. Others are less certain about the Filioque's ultimate significance for theology and life. However, all agree that the Filioque is a major issue of debate which, if resolved, would prove a dramatic step forward in the ecumenical struggle toward unity.

1. A COMMON CONFESSION OF THE TRINITY

The right starting point for a discussion of the Filioque against the background of the trinitarian doctrine is an acknowledgment of a common confession of faith in the Holy Trinity by the eastern and western churches. Great Church fathers such as Athanasius, Basil and Gregory Nanzianzus who were deeply involved in the trinitarian controversies of the fourth century, as well as later Church fathers such as Maximus the Confessor and Gregory Palamas who are also authoritative for eastern Orthodox theology, not infrequently raise the issue of the *overall intention* or *meaning* of theological discourse. The trinitarian and chris-

23

tological debates were not over words as if these had sacrosanct value. Gregory Palamas was ready to accept the language of procession of the Spirit from the Son as well as the Father, if such procession was correctly interpreted. Maximus the Confessor has in fact provided an Orthodox interpretation of the Filioque. Athanasius counselled brotherly acceptance of Orthodox bishops who held to the saving truth about the Son but could not in good faith accept the canonical term *homoousios* (of the same essence) decreed by the First Council at Nicea (325). The central question was, and always is, whether or not the faith of the universal Church, as revealed in Scripture and recited in the baptismal confession and the worship of the Church, is proclaimed.

In our debate about the Filioque, the warning that we, too, should take care not to argue over words has tremendous implications both for Christian brotherhood and theological accuracy. Disputants usually regard as burning issues their differences which they tend to evaluate somewhat out of context. That is why we must begin with our common confession of faith in the mystery of the Holy Trinity recited in prayer, worship and the Creed. By wide agreement the main source of the western teaching of the Filioque is Augustine's work *On the Trinity* (e.g., iv, 20; xv, 26-27). But Augustine clearly intended to uphold the faith of the Church and submitted to the authority of both Church and Ecumenical Councils. He in no way sided with Sabellian, Arian or Eunomian teachings, which he rejected, but in good conscience confessed the Catholic faith (*de Trin.* i, 4; xv, 28). If, then, a common confession in the Trinity, one God in three distinct persons, Father, Son and Holy Spirit, is acknowledged, is the Filioque (*a*) a matter of theological speculation (*theologoumenon*), (*b*) an alternative interpretation of the trinitarian doctrine or (*c*) an heretical teaching damaging Christian truth as dangerously as one of the ancient heresies?

2. SINGLE OR DOUBLE PROCESSION

Where the article on the Holy Spirit in the Creed, completed at the Second Ecumenical Council (381), states that the Spirit 'proceeds from (*ek*) the Father', it does so paralleling the article on the Son which states that the Son is 'begotten of (*ek*) the Father'. These credal expressions of the First and Second Councils, and the theology of the Church fathers behind them, hold that the Father is the cause of the procession of the Spirit just as the Father is the cause of the generation of the Son. The problem lies here: the addition of the Filioque alters the Creed to state that the Spirit 'proceeds from the Father *and (from) the Son*', promulgating not a single procession of the Spirit from the Father but a double procession of the Spirit from the Father and the Son. What is the difference?

1. *The Terminology: Generation and Procession*

The terms 'generation' (*gennesis*) and 'procession' (*ekporeusis*), which have a biblical background (John 1:18; 15:26; Ps. 2:7), are not decisive in themselves. *Athanasius* and the three *Cappadocians* (Basil, Gregory Nanzianzus and Gregory Nyssa), the foremost exponents and defenders of the Nicene faith, whose writings are crucial for the correct interpretation of the doctrinal formulations of the two Councils, point out that we cannot know by rational speculation what the eternal generation of the Son or the eternal procession of the Spirit are. What we can know by deduction from revelation is *that* they are and that they are *different* because the Son and the Spirit are distinct (for example, the Son alone was incarnate). By adopting the term 'procession' (*ekporeusis*) the Second Council intended to affirm the individuality of the Holy Spirit. Thus the synodal letter of the same Council, using Basil's differentiation between *ousia* (essence) and *hypostasis* (person) affirmed the unity (*homoousion*) of God in three perfect *hypostaseis* (persons) and explicitly cautioned not to confuse the *hypostaseis* by abolishing their individual properties (*idiotētes*).

2. *The Properties*

What are these individual properties? In the writings of the above Church fathers the matter is frequently addressed. While the three persons of the Trinity are completely united having the same honour, glory, power and essence, they are also distinguished by the following incommunicable properties: the Father is unbegotten, the cause and caused by no other in the Trinity; the Son is begotten of the Father, and the Holy Spirit proceeds from the Father. Unbegottenness or paternity, generation or sonship, and proceeding or procession are the individual properties which must be posited to safeguard the distinct eternal existence of each person of the Trinity. The three divine persons are completely united in essence, honour and action but are distinguished *only* by their individual properties. They abide in each other, belong to each other and share all things in common. What they absolutely do not share are exactly those individual properties which eternally distinguish them in their mode of *individual* existence as Father, Son and Holy Spirit. Thus, while the Son and Spirit simultaneously derive from the Father, they do so in a different manner because they are distinct. There is only one Son, who was incarnate, and he derives his eternal existence from the Father by generation; there is only one Spirit and he derives his eternal existence from the Father by procession, while the Father himself is distinct from both in that he derives from no one but is the cause of both Son and Spirit. On the basis of these terms, the Filioque compromises the individual property of the Father as the unbegotten and only cause within the Trinity. To teach according to the Filioque that the Spirit proceeds also from the Son in any sense that the Son also *causes* the eternal existence of the Spirit is to confuse the individual properties of the persons of the Trinity.

3. *The Alternative Terminology of Augustine*

However, the Filioque cannot immediately be measured by the above terms because it derives from another context. Augustine, the intellectual father of the Filioque, was aware of the distinction between essence and *hypostasis* (person) in God but he did not by his own admission quite understand it (*de Trin.* v, 8). He clearly distinguished between the generation of the Son and the procession of the Spirit, but was confused about why the Spirit who is also derived from the Father is not another 'Son' because Augustine thought that the manner of generation and the manner of procession might possibly be rationally explained (although he in the end admitted that he was himself unable to do it; xv, 24 and 26). He states that the Father is the beginning (*principium,* iv, 20) within the Trinity, that the Spirit proceeds *principally* from the Father (xv, 26) but finally that the Spirit proceeds from both the Father and the Son as from a single beginning or source (v, 14; xv, 27). But he does not then say how generation and procession can really be different. Thus, while affirming throughout his work the unity as well as the *individuality* of the persons of the Trinity, Augustine nevertheless unsuspectingly confuses their individual properties according to the terminology of the Second Council. We have here a paradox: in his overall intention Augustine upholds the Catholic faith but his language regarding the double procession of the Spirit from the Father as well as the Son, in their eternal individual existence, is inadequate by the standards of the Second Council and the theology behind it.

3. DIFFERENT THEOLOGICAL APPROACHES

For any hopeful breakthrough in the debate over the Filioque, the investigation must move beyond simple comparison of the Filioque and the terminology of the Second Council into consideration of the entire theological approaches behind them and of what in these approaches are crucial divergencies. In this regard three observations are important regarding style, historical context and doctrinal value.

1. *Different Style*

By style is meant the character and spirit of theological exposition. That Augustine's is philosophical whereas Athanasius' and the Cap-

padocians' is biblical, as sometimes claimed, is not true without qualification. All of these Church fathers use Scripture as their ultimate
authority. They all employ an intellectual discursive exposition which
includes formal terms and notions such as essence, *hypostasis,* immutability, time, eternity, act according to essence, act according to will and
the like. Significantly, Augustine's teaching of the Filioque is derived
more from biblical texts, such as John 15:26; 20:22 (*de Trin.* iv, 20) and
Gal. 4:6 (xv, 26), as well as from the biblical principle that the Son has
whatever the Father has (xv, 26-27), rather than from his philosophical
interpretations of the Trinity. After all Augustine himself not infrequently states that his reflections about the Trinity are based on the data
of faith and not the reverse. The difference seems to be that, despite his
own repeated reservations, Augustine is almost naively bold about what
can be conceived of the inner life of the Trinity, gives himself to speculation in terms of several human analogies and ends his book in a pray-
erful tentative mood by stressing the difficulties in the intellectual task of
understanding the Trinity (xv, chaps. 2, 5, 22-24, 28). He gives the
impression of presenting his thoughts as a kind of personal theological
speculation about the Trinity resting on the security of the Church's
dogma about the Trinity.

2. Different Historical Context

But the case is different with Athanasius and the Cappadocians. While
philosophically more sensitive to the incomprehensibility of the essence
of God, they firmly argue about the truth of the Church's revealed faith in
terms of basic principles which are at stake. They neither give themselves
to open speculation, nor do they seek to understand the inner life of the
Trinity on the basis of faith, but unhesitatingly they defend the Catholic
faith against heretics. If the Son is Saviour, how can he be created? If the
son is uncreated, he cannot be related to the Father in the same way as the
world is related to God because the world is a creation. Is the Spirit
created or uncreated? How can both the unity and trinitarian nature of
God be defended against heretical teaching that compromised one aspect
or the other? Such were their questions. The crucial *historical* factor is
this: Athanasius, the Cappadocians and many other fathers who wrote in
Greek shared an ongoing debate—an entire historical context of issues,
terms, principles, biblical interpretations, Councils and writings of
Church fathers and heretics. After a long and hard-won struggle, they
hammered out an impressive consensus on the Trinity which involved
definite terminology and clear principles. But Augustine was removed
from this context. The problem was not geography or time. Augustine
simply was not at home with Greek, as he admits. Unable to read in depth
the extensive writings of Church fathers and heretics not yet available in

Latin translation, Augustine never became integrally rooted in the above trinitarian consensus. While accepting both the Catholic faith and the decrees of the Councils, his gifted mind simply set out on a different path.

3. *Different Doctrinal Value*

The matter of doctrinal value is most crucial. If the above remarks are in the main true, then Augustine's teaching of the Filioque has the value of personal theological meditation. It probably cannot even be regarded as a serious alternative interpretation of the Trinity because it does not really take into account the standard interpretation of the Church fathers and Councils hammered out on the anvil of the actual struggle against Sabellianism, Arianism and Eunomianism. Above all Augustine's teaching cannot be viewed as the *normative* teaching of the Church. The only normative teaching about the Trinity is that of the Ecumenical Councils against the background of the trinitarian theology of the Church fathers mentioned above who were the Catholic principals in the trinitarian controversy with the ancient heresies.

Although Augustine unknowingly set a different path, one may still ask what the important divergencies are in trinitarian teaching between him and the Greek fathers. The *heart of the problem* is that Augustine's views, not sharpened by full knowledge of the struggle against the ancient heresies, lack a fundamental theological principle which emerged as a first line of defence against Arianism, namely, that the manner by which the Father 'causes' the existence of the uncreated *Son* and uncreated *Spirit* is *radically different from* that by which the entire Trinity 'causes' the created *world* and manifests Itself in it. The former involves the essence of God and the eternal existence of the Holy Trinity (God in Himself), while the latter involves the will of God and the Trinity's revelation in time and history (God with us). Applied to the former, the Filioque is *unacceptable* for reasons already stated. Applied to the latter the Filioque is *acceptable* according to Maximus the Confessor's interpretation because the entire Trinity shares a common will, action, glory, kingdom and grace, just as the Trinity shares a common essence. Excepting the single case of the incarnation of the Son, which is according to the eternal person of the Son and not only according to the will of the Trinity, all other manifestations of God are absolutely common: the Father always acts through the Son in the Holy Spirit. In this sense, the Spirit who abides in and belongs to the Son (Gal. 4:6) also proceeds from and is sent to the world (John 15:26) by the Son who is the agent of creation, revelation and redemption. But the Son does not cause the eternal existence of the Spirit. Thus when Jesus imparts the Spirit to the apostles (John 20:20), he does not impart to them the *hypostasis* (person) but the grace of the Holy Spirit which is common to Father, Son and Spirit.

The above differentiation between the Trinity's eternal inner existence and volitional activity toward the world is impossible unless God's essence and will are distinguished, as they are by Athanasius and the Cappadocians against the Arians. This is the crucial distinction of 'essence' and 'energies' in God on which Orthodox theologians insist in order to maintain both the personal immanence of God in his creation as well as his radical difference from it. God is one, yet revealed and hidden; partially revealed by his will or activity, absolutely hidden in his inner being or essence. This distinction, far from negating the simplicity of God who is perfect and present at all times and in all places according to both essence and will, affirms the biblical faith in the living God of Abraham, Isaac and Jacob who acts in creation and history, has personal communion with human beings in prayer, sacrament and righteous living, while he remains ineffably transcendent in himself. At this level of doctrinal interpretation the Filioque becomes a matter about the truth of God as revealed to us and about our relations with him—a matter of salvation.

4. UNCANONICAL ADDITION

Not least important is the canonical question of the addition of the Filioque to the Creed against the authority of the Ecumenical Councils. This is not merely a legal question but one that touches on the unanimity and catholicity of the Church. The Creed includes an article of faith regarding 'the One, Holy, Catholic and Apostolic Church'. The highest voice of this Church is expressed in Ecumenical Councils. How can the unanimity of the Church stand if the Ecumenical Councils are disregarded? The insertion of the Filioque violates the bond of love that holds the entire Church together. If one local Church acts arbitrarily, is not the common trust broken by which all agree to walk together regarding the most essential matters of faith as commonly decided in Ecumenical Councils?

Had the Filioque been raised at an Ecumenical Council, an inevitable encounter and interaction with the trinitarian theology of the First and Second Councils would have occurred. A possible solution in the direction of Maximus the Confessor's interpretation of the Filioque might then have been officially adopted. But as events turned out, one side acted arbitrarily, attributed canonical status to theological speculation not in complete harmony with the theology of the Ecumenical Councils and tried in vain to impose it on the eastern churches. On all counts the Filioque significantly deepened the ongoing estrangement of the western and eastern churches and became a sign of western error and presumptuousness.

5. CONCLUSION

The Filioque is not a decisive difference in dogma but a serious difference in the interpretation of dogma which awaits resolution. Prior to the recitation of the Creed in the Eucharist, the following prayer is offered: 'Let us love one another that we may with one mind confess: Father, Son and Holy Spirit, Trinity consubstantial and indivisible.' The tragedy of the Filioque is that, while not intended as a denial of the Catholic faith, and while yielding to an Orthodox interpretation, it nonetheless gained a controversial significance beyond the imagination of Augustine because of a differing theology, subsequent ecclesiastical acts and the eventual great schism between the western and eastern churches. Today theologians have to deal with the historical consciousness of the separated churches as much as with the Filioque as a theological issue.

In the struggle sensitively to differentiate and properly to deal with the various aspects of the debate, *exaggerated and uncritical claims must be avoided*. For example, that the Filioque subordinates the Spirit to the Son and leads to a subordination of the Church to the pope (as the vicar of Christ) is a polemical and false Orthodox interpretation. The Filioque became a sign (for the eastern Church) of papal absolutism, not the cause of it. Again, that the Filioque is an expression of a theology that brought about the secularisation of western society is a sweeping thesis by some Orthodox theologians which overlooks other major factors (e.g., the rise of modern science, industrialisation, mass media and the like). But *western theologians, too, are seriously challenged* in several ways. They must declare themselves on the trinitarian theology of the First and Second Ecumenical Councils. Is this the normative trinitarian teaching of the Church or not? They must reflect on whether the Augustinian premise of rationally explaining the data of faith has not in part led western theology, either in its scholastic or modern liberal forms, to subtle but deep shifts away from the spirit and authority of Scripture and the Catholic tradition. For example, are the theophanies of God in the Bible (e.g., to Moses, Isaiah and St Paul), as well as man's communion with God in prayer, liturgy and Christian living, real or not, and what are the consequent implications in terms of doctrinal explication? Finally they must consider the removal of the Filioque from the Creed both for the sake of the Catholic bond of love and with the anticipation that a future Ecumenical Council could very well incorporate the Filioque into the Creed in mutually acceptable terms.

Part II

Word and Spirit:
The Question of the Reformation

Inge Lønning

The Reformation and
the Enthusiasts

1. THE CONDEMNATION OF THE ENTHUSIASTS:
NO FAITH WITHOUT THE BODILY WORD OF THE GOSPEL

According to the Confession of Augsburg (1530), 'The anabaptists and others who teach that we can attain to the Holy Spirit without the bodily word of the gospel and through our own preparation, thoughts and work are condemned' (article 5). This is one of the most central passages in what is perhaps the most important theological pronouncement of the Reformation and certainly the Protestant document that is most strongly marked by history and tradition. This sharp condemnation is, moreover, the reverse side of a carefully defined dogmatic position in which at least six different elements can be distinguished.

These are, firstly, faith, which is defined in article 4 as the faith of the one who believes 'that Christ suffered for us and that for his sake sin is forgiven and justice and eternal life is given'. According to the Confession of Augsburg, moreover, the only author of this faith is the Spirit of God. Secondly, both the Spirit and the faith brought about by that Spirit are the gift of God and both are irreducible and inexplicable. In the third place, this gift is, in accordance with God's will, mediated through the service of the Church, in other words, through the gospel and the sacrament. Fourthly, the gospel of the grace of God in Christ must encounter man in a bodily form, from outside. Fifthly, the audible proclamation of the Word and the visible sacramental acts are necessary but not sufficient as pre-conditions for this faith that is brought about primarily by the Spirit, because—and this is the sixth element that can be distinguised—the freedom of God is beyond the power of the one who receives the Spirit to understand and cannot in any way be restricted.

Many historical problems are raised in this context. We cannot unfortunately consider here the problem of who these 'anabaptists and others' were and whether their theological position was clearly defined or not. What concerns us above all is the simple fact that the theology of the Reformation, for which the Confession of Augsburg must be regarded as an authoritative document, is placed in a relationship of irreconcilable contrast with regard to a spiritualised conception of the Spirit and faith. The decisive criterion of the doctrine of the Church is seen, within this relationship, in the theological adherence to the 'bodily word' (in the Latin version of the text, the *verbum externum*). Anyone who separates faith—and therefore the Spirit who brings about that faith—from the medium of this bodily word is promulgating a doctrine that places him outside the Church. The Church only exists because the Spirit and the bodily word were brought together in accordance with God's will and belong together for eternity.

This dividing line was not drawn arbitrarily, since it was regarded as important at the Diet of Augsburg in 1530 to be dissociated from certain politically dangerous movements of a revolutionary kind. It was, then, a consistent and even necessary definition. The bodily or external nature of the gospel is indissolubly connected with the very matter of the gospel. If faith were able to come about without the bodily word of the gospel, then it ought to be possible to find the gospel in one way or another within the possibilities of human thought. The need for a bodily proclamation of the word and a bodily sacramental action can be directly inferred from the external nature of Christ's work of salvation. Just as that work was accomplished from outside and before believing man, so too can the fruits of that work of salvation—according to the Augsburg Confession, article 4, the forgiveness of sins, justice and eternal life—only be received from outside, that is, bodily.

The Spirit, the word and faith are clearly brought together here in an indissoluble and dynamic unity. The theological necessity of the anathema pronounced against the enthusiasts can be traced back to the indissolubility of this unity. Anyone who denies the mediation of the Spirit who brings about faith through the audible world of the sermon and the visible action of the sacraments is in fact replacing the function of the Spirit in bringing about faith with the creative power of the human spirit. To claim that faith and the reception of the Spirit are possible without the medium of the bodily word or *verbum externum* is to deny that the Church's ministry was instituted by God.

This clear definition, marking the Reformers' teaching about the Spirit, the word and faith from a spiritualised view, places the Confession of Augsburg firmly within the tradition of the greater Church. According to article 5 of the Confession, it is obviously not simply permitted, but also dogmatically imposed on believers to think of the Church in its social, bodily form as an *institutio Dei*. The rather strange wording of the article, however—'institutum est ministerium ecclesiasticum/God has instituted the office of preaching'—shows that the relationship between pneumatology and ecclesiology was understood differently from the way in which it had hitherto been understood in the tradition of the Church.

This definition of the Church's ministry, as found in the Confession of Augsburg, also exists at two levels. On the one hand, it explicitly marks off the conviction of the Reformers from the spiritualised pneumatology of the enthusiasts. On the other hand, however, it also implicitly marks off their teaching from the pneumatology of the Roman tradition with its strong emphasis on canon law. The Spirit is not, in other words, tied to the Church as a hierarchical institution, but to the bodily word of the gospel in baptism, preaching and the Lord's Supper.

2. THE REFORMATION BETWEEN THE LEFT AND THE RIGHT?
QUESTIONS ABOUT A SCHEME OF INTERPRETATION

Turning now to the contemporary theological scene, it is obvious that the ecumenical problem is almost entirely determined by our acceptance nowadays of the co-existence of many Christian confessions or churches as a matter of course. It is equally clear to us today that we can only do justice to the reality if we make use of careful comparative methods. In this process, it is possible to use, with certain modifications, the scheme of interpretation according to left and right wing that is usually employed in the political sciences and apply it to a systematic classification of the individual denominations. Elements of systematic theology and empirical sociology are inextricably linked in the criteria used in this process of classification. On the left wing, there are, for example, the spiritualistic communities of the charismatic type and, on the right wing, there is, of course, the Church as a hierarchical institution. The main structural criterion is the question of legal organisation and the contrast between the Spirit and the institution of the Church.

In all probability, the churches of the Reformation should be placed in a central position in this scheme of interpretation. In the Lutheran theological tradition, this position has frequently been ideologised to the extent that the Church in the centre is seen as the original, authentic and orthodox Church following the golden middle way, undisturbed by all the left- and right-wing theological movements. This conception of the Church in the middle position has resulted, in the Church's understanding of itself, in a strange methodological convention in the question of presenting its own tradition in Christian teaching. It is, in other words, only by defining its boundaries to the left and the right that the Church can make its own position quite clear. A repeated emphasis on the two extreme wings can act as an indispensable means of support in the Church's understanding and presentation of itself.

It is clear, moreover, that a confessional accentuation of the Church's position can also be valuable from the ecumenical point of view. The Church has a potential part to play as a mediator because of its position midway between the left and the right.

This scheme based on the left and right wings is not simply the result of systematic contemporary research into the positions occupied by the different Christian confessions. From the very beginning of the Reformation, this same idea of the two wings has always played an important part. The whole historical development of the Reformation can be seen, at least from Luther's point of view, as a strategical game. The sequence of events from 1517 (Luther's theses on indulgences) until 1521 (Luther's defence of his teachings at the Diet of Worms) led to the formation of a front line against Rome. A second front was opened in 1525 with the publication of the controversial treatise 'Against the heavenly prophets' (*Wider die himmlischen Propheten*) and this occupied the centre of interest in the years that followed. The whole history of the Reformation should be seen in terms of a war on two fronts and the main interest in this war is the shift in the centre of gravity.

The historical and the systematic schemes of interpretation therefore bear each other out. Luther recognised that he was compelled to affirm his teaching when challenged by enemies on the right and enemies on the left. In the same way, later Lutheran theologians have always had to defend the theology that they have inherited against enemies both on the right and on the left wing.

This is not, however, in accordance with Luther's own understanding of theology. On the contrary, in 1535, after ten years of war on two fronts—according to the scheme of interpretation outlined above—Luther declared with unmistakable clarity in the preface to his great commentary on Galatians that there was only one theological front. On the one side of this front line, there was, in his opinion, the *Ecclesia Dei* and, on the other side, the papists and the anabaptists, who were united. According to the external impression, an irreconcilable enmity existed between the two, but in fact they were completely united with regard to their teaching. (Luther's own words are: 'Fingunt enim sese foris magnos hostes illorum, cum tamen intus vere idem sentiant, doceant ac defendant contra unicum illum salvatorem Christum qui solus est iustitia nostra': *Gesammelte Werke, Weimarer Ausgabe* 40, I, 36).

We must now turn our attention to this challenging assertion.

3. THE FALSE DOCTRINE:
QUOD OPUS DIVINUM PENDEAT EX DIGNITATE PERSONAE

Luther is concerned, in the preface to his commentary on the Epistle to the Galatians, with the *petra ecclesiae*, the foundation of the Church. With an unmistakable allusion to Paul's way of expressing himself in 1 Cor. 3, Luther speaks of the only effective foundation which 'we call *locus iustificationis*'. He defines the content of this foundation in a way that is reminiscent of the definition of faith in article 4 of the Confession of Augsburg: '*Hoc est, quomodo non per nos ipsos (haud dubie neque per opera nostra, quae minus quam nos ipsi), sed per alienum auxilium, per Filium unigenitum Dei, Iesum Christum, simus a peccato, morte, Diabolo redempti et vita aeterna donati.*' This foundation has been disputed from the time of creation onwards by the devil, Luther insisted, just as man's foundation in his own strength and wisdom has been challenged since he abandoned trust in God.

It is hardly possible to extend the horizon further in order to come to terms theologically with the enthusiasts. It is, on the other hand, quite possible to pursue our thinking further from the fundamental alternative, *locus iustificationis* or self-assertion, to which we have already referred, to the presumably structurally similar and contemporary alternative. The enthusiasts denied the foundation of the Church in their teaching that God's work of salvation depended on the religious quality of those who believed in him. Luther used the example of baptism to illustrate this denial: '*Sic enim docent Anabaptistae: Baptisma nihil est, nisi persona sit credens. Ex hoc principio (ut dicitur) necesse est sequi, omnia opera Dei nihil esse, si homo non sit bonus. Baptisma autem est opus Dei, sed homo malus facit, ut non sit opus Dei*' (WA 40, I, 36).

This argument is clearly anti-Donatistic and as such is almost indistinguishable from the polemics of the same period directed by the Roman Catholic Church against the enthusiasts. Luther's anti-Donatism is, however, theologically distinctive in that he equates the doctrine of the religious quality of the individual believer with the legally based doctrine of the succession of office. Apart from this, it is not possible to understand the inclusion of both positions under the same heading of *dignitas personae*. Just as the anabaptists linked the saving reality of God in the sacrament directly to the faith of the individual as a precondition for receiving the sacrament, so too was a connection made between the doctrine of the sacrament of ordination and the personal dignity of the legally ordained office-bearer. As Luther points out: '*Conspirant namque Papistae et Anabaptistae hodie in unam hanc sententiam concorditer contra ecclesiam Dei (etiamsi dissimulent verbo) quod opus divinum pendeat ex dignitate personae*' (WA 40, I, 36).

The witness borne by the Church of the Reformation to the Holy Spirit can best be understood in the light of the doctrine of justification as the *articulus stantis et cadentis ecclesiae*. Pneumatology is a doctrine of the God who justifies the godless in Christ. It is not something different from or additional to this. The doctrine of the Spirit, then, should be understood in the light of our knowledge of God and man as expressed by Luther in his exposition of Psalm 51 (1532): '*Cognitio dei et hominis est sapientia divina et proprie theologica. Et ita cognitio dei et hominis, ut referatur tandem ad deum iustificantem et hominem peccatorem, ut proprie sit subiectum Theologiae homo reus et perditus et deus iustificans vel salvator, quidquid extra istud argumentum vel subiectum quaeritur, hoc plane est error et vanitas in Theologia*' (WA 40, II, 327f). Any pneumatology that results in any other conclusion, is, in other words, a false doctrine.

What is Luther asserting, then, in identifying these two apparently opposite positions in this way? He is simply saying that the attempt to link the Spirit to the personal dignity of the individual in each case results in a misunderstanding of the one theme of theology. On the basis of this single theme of theology, all that can be said about the Spirit of God is that the justification of the sinner is expressed as the creative activity of God. The Spirit brings about faith in Christ not through the medium of man's inner experience, the charismatic bearers of the Spirit or the legal power of the bearers of office in the Church, but through the bodily word of the gospel. We may therefore say that the Church of Christ also brings about this faith through the bodily word.

It is therefore not a question of a central position between spiritualism and pneumatic institutionalism, but of the one front line set up in opposition to the definition of the Spirit as the Spirit of office in the Church, in other words, of those holding office, or to the Spirit of the believers themselves. The alternative definition here is: the Spirit of the bodily word.

4. THE OFFICE OF PREACHING AND THE BODILY WORD OF THE GOSPEL

To speak of a *verbum externum* is, of course, to presuppose the existence of a *verbum internum* and the validity of the anthropological distinction between the external and the inner man. What is important here is the way in which this distinction is applied. The decisive question for any theological anthropology is: What are the consequences of this distinction for our understanding of man's relationship with God? The same question can also be differently phrased: How can the need for this distinction be deduced from man's relationship with God?

If what we have here is a distinction that is indispensable to our correct understanding of man, then it is not possible to divide man into two parts and to identify his relationship with God with one part of him. The consequences for our understanding of the central theological concepts of creation and salvation of an identification of the function of the Spirit of God with the inner life of man as something completely separate from his bodily nature would certainly be disastrous. The philosophical contrast between spirit and matter therefore replaced the theological contrast between spirit and sin, the important contrast being no longer that between the Holy Spirit and lack of faith or man as a sinner, but that between the Holy Spirit and man's bodily nature. In this, however, faith had inevitably to be understood as the spiritual potential of the inner man.

The gospel appeals to man in his receptivity rather than his creativity. This is expressed in the clearly defined movement from outside to inside, that is, from the *verbum externum* to the *verbum internum*. The *verbum externum* is an audible phenomenon, a factor that can be ascertained intersubjectively. That the *verbum externum* may possibly become a *verbum internum* which determines man's entire person is a process that lies outside the sphere of human reflection. According to article 5 of the Augsburg Confession, the Holy Spirit brings about faith in men who hear the bodily word of the gospel *ubi et quando visum est Deo*.

As an *institutio Dei,* the Church's ministry has clearly to be understood as God's grace and as his blessing and gift. It is also something that is indissolubly linked with Christ's work of salvation. The Spirit distributes the saving work of Christ to God's fallen creature, man, through the bodily nature of the proclamation of the word and the sacramental actions. It is not a part of man, but man as a whole who is justified. Justification cannot be achieved by the partial justice of our own performances. Man can only be made just in God's sight by the justice of Christ that is received from outside. Faith is therefore dependent on the ministry of the Church, which promises the believer Christ's justice through baptism, preaching and the Lord's Supper.

What we have in fact described in this article is the bodily character of the Christian form of public worship. According to the Confession of Augsburg, article 7, the Church is defined as *'congregatio sanctorum, in qua pure docetur evangelium et recte administrantur sacramenta'*. This definition applies to the Christian community assembled for worship. This aspect is even more clearly expressed in a translation of the German version of the same article: 'The assembly of all believers in which the gospel is preached in a pure form and the sacraments are administered in accordance with the gospel'.

The Spirit of God is active in this bodily assembly of believers and arouses, nourishes and perfects faith, in this way taking God's work with his creation to its end. The Church, as the assembly of all believers, is sustained by the office of preaching, in other words, by the promise of the gospel in baptism, the sermon and the Lord's Supper. God has linked his Spirit to the office of preaching. In conclusion, we may therefore say that there is one front only in the pneumatological teaching of the Reformed Church, but that this has two distinct emphases. The first is the *bodily* word of the Spirit and the second is the bodily *word* of the Spirit.

Translated by David Smith

John H. Yoder

The Enthusiasts and
the Reformation

THE TERM 'enthusiast' is one of the few terms of abuse from the sixteenth century for which a more technical substitute has still not been found. One possibility would be to rehabilitate the term by giving it a technical definition.[1] This would involve (see below) a specific concept of the action of the Holy Spirit, but this more precise description would cover only a few of the individuals and movements traditionally designated by the term.

The other possible method in historical description, and the one chosen in this volume, is to abandon the particular pneumatological content just mentioned and use 'enthusiast' to refer to the whole motley range of renewal movements in the century which were not recognised by the state. However the logical cost of this extension of the definition is that the resulting collective term no longer has any content. 'Enthusiasm' never existed. Neither sociologically nor theologically can such an entity be identified. Really the only feature common to all the individuals gathered under the cover term was that they did not win (or refused to seek) the support of the local ruler for their alternative forms of religious renewal. We shall therefore be obliged to analyse a number of concepts of the spirit with the open admission that differently structured typologies would be equally possible. The word 'Spirit' will rarely be the only or the standard word used in the description; often the same idea can be expressed by 'Lord' or 'Word'.

1. THE SPIRIT AS A PRINCIPLE OF UNCONTROLLABLE INSPIRATION

Spiritus jactant, 'They boast of the Spirit', was Huldrych Zwingli's judgment on the people he called *catabaptistes*. The description is not

41

accurate, at least not as a technical description of those of his former disciples who had created the Baptist free church movement.[2] Nevertheless to treat the Holy Spirit as a principle of uncontrollable inspiration was and remains a possible view and one which has supporters. In the cases of Wolfgang Uolimann or Augustin Bader on the fringe of the Baptist movement,[3] in that of Magdalena Müller of St Gallen, who returned to the state Church, or in that of the mad Leonhard Schugger such an understanding was an important element. These extremes were few in number, but so striking that it was easy for the polemicists of the state churches to present them as typical. This is perhaps also the context in which a technical definition of 'genuine enthusiasm' would be of value. In the nature of things such people did not form lasting movements, did not develop bodies of doctrine and did not enter into discussions with others.

2. THE SPIRIT AS THE SEAL OF A NEW AGE

'Spirit' can also be taken in a Joachimite or even Montanist sense to imply the mark of a new age transcending the earlier stages of salvation history represented by the incarnation and the Church. Developments in both devotion and economics and politics in the decades of the reformation aroused new tensions and hopes which were bound to be disappointed by the ('spiritlessly') sober results of the ecclesiastical reformation and created a demand for something more. This could take various forms.

1. The 'more' thus sought for could be the work of the Spirit in the sense that in terms of a pre-reformation ascetic and mystical view 'the Spirit' is the sign and source of inner authenticity as an alternative to reason and force. Such accents can be heard in Hans Denck and the early Thomas Müntzer. The Spirit illuminates, gives the believer the assurance of his own election, clarifies the sense of otherwise contradictory writings and leads the individual to grasp and deepen his or her own salvation.

2. Similar and yet different is the effect of the concept of the Spirit among the so-called 'Spiritualists'. Here the term stands less for a guiding force than for a metaphysical principle in polarity with the fleshly, the visible and the external. With or without Platonic language, theologians are anxious to emphasise distance. Caspar von Schwenckenfeld took the trouble to work out his own dogmatics, with a characteristic doctrine of the eucharist (welcomed by Zwingli in 1528) and christology (based on the concept of the 'heavenly flesh' of Christ). The ecclesiastical result of such elevated perspectives was a relativisation of the disputes about any matter of external organisation. Why should anyone bother so much

about a reform of the visible? Sebastian Franck, the author of a famous universal history, distanced himself from all parties of whatever tendency: whether 'popish, Lutheran, Zwinglian or Anabaptist', all were to be rejected for their dogmatism and concern with forms. In their description of true interiority the spiritualists are quite close to the mystics, though they have their own interest in an absence of dogmatism and a universal culture which makes them look more like precursors of the enlightenment, while someone like Hans Denck still belongs more to the middle ages. The 'Spirit' is thinner, its effects less powerful and less associated with scripture and prophecy.

3. Melchior Hofmann, who caused serious disorder in the Netherlands by introducing adult baptism, was not a true 'enthusiast' in the sense of claiming illuminations or prophetic revelations of his own, though he was uncritical in accepting the prophecies of others. He himself claimed only to be an interpreter of holy scripture. His main writings are commentaries. Correct interpretation, however, requires, in his view, various particular hermeneutical keys, and it is the Holy Spirit who has given Hofmann the insights which provide these. He claimed that his proclamation of the imminent end of the world was based, not in inspiration, but on an objectively correct exegesis which unlocked the meaning of the biblical documents.

4. In spite of the variety of the starting-points, these various tendencies share a certain lack of definition, or an openness towards the future. They all attach little importance to tradition. They all expect an extension or deepening of the reformation, which is still in its beginnings. It is the preparation for the next step, the outpouring of the Holy Spirit as the appearance of the eschatological kingdom of God. Without violence, and even in suffering, as long as the hour of redemption had not struck (according to Hofmann himself and Hans Hut), the apocalyptic thinker looked forward to great social upheavals, not unconnected with the urban and rural disorders of the period. The move to this next step can thus be made from a more mystical position (1) as in the case of the later Thomas Müntzer, from the erratic biblicism of Hofmann's heirs (Münster 1534-35), or from the position of a genuinely naive enthusiast like Augustin Bader. It was these excesses which echoed down through the pages of both secular and ecclesiastical history for centuries. They created the picture of the 'enthusiast' as a larger-than-life visionary who proves by his lack of restraint that the sober mainstream of the reformation is right to preserve the continuity of doctrinal tradition and state supervision.

3. THE SPIRIT AS THE PRINCIPLE OF AUTHORITY IN THE COMMUNITY

The career of the idea of the Spirit in primitive Protestant congregationalism is quite different. Both Luther and Zwingli in 1523 asserted the authority of the assembled local community (or of a synod or a council, but that was not then the issue), to take binding decisions on matters of truth, life and Church order without consulting distant hierarchs. The argument for this authority was provided by the model presented in 1 Cor. 14, where every member has the right to speak and all the others listen and make a critical evaluation, and the account in Acts 15, where the result of a similarly structured discussion was a consensus. Unanimity is itself a sign of the action of the Holy Spirit (15:23). Initially the reformers assumed that the authorities on the spot, as part of the unity created by the Spirit, would act as an executive organ to implement the decisions taken, since one of the tasks of the reformation was to find a substitute for episcopal control. Soon, however, assembled local communities began to come into conflict with the city authorities.

In October 1523 an elaborate assembly in Zurich summoned to judge on a disputation found in favour of Zwingli's views on the eucharist and the worship of images. The question arose whether the council ('my lords') or the assembly itself should give legal force to the newly won truths. Zwingli was ready to leave it to the council.

At this Simon Stumpf said, 'You have no power to hand over judgment to my lords. The judgment has already been given. The Spirit of God judges'.

By this the radical Zwinglian meant quite literally, 'Our present assembly has reached a decision which must be regarded as the work of the Spirit and therefore as final'. Zwingli agreed. 'My lords' should merely settle the details of the implementation of the decision. In Zwingli's view too, the council had no right to say anything about the truth of God's word, which had now been correctly interpreted.

But 'my lords' had their own views about their responsibilities as constitutents of the Church. They kept the reformer waiting a long time for the implementation of the decision. Problems of this sort were to result in the disintegration of the Zwinglian reformation. Its radical branch was prepared to accept congregationalism even if this meant forgoing the co-operation of the authorities, and ended in the Baptist free church movement. Zwingli, on the other hand, continued to accept the executive authority of the council as the presbyterium of the city community. He allowed the idea of the unity produced by the Spirit in the community assembled under the proclaimed word to remain theoretical for the future, though it was to be influential later with Bucer, Calvin and in puritanism.

The breakthrough to a viable organisation was made in the Baptist movement of the Upper Rhine in Schlechtheim in February 1527.[4] The agreement reached 'without the opposition of any brother and to universal satisfaction' was regarded as a proof of the action of the Holy Spirit in a Trinitarian framework: 'In all this we have felt that the unity of the Father and of Christ who binds us all together has been with us, together with their Spirit.' Subjects of the negotiations and 'brotherly settlement' were specific problems of order (baptism, the eucharist, excommunication, the pastoral office) and social ethics (the sword, oaths). This is the first time in the century of the reformation that a common community structure was discovered capable of surviving without or (unfortunately usually) in opposition to the civil power.

4. THE SPIRIT AS THE FORCE OF SUBJECTIVE APPROPRIATION OF THE TRUTH

Complementary to the congregational concept, but not simply identical with it, is the concept of the Spirit as the power of subjective appropriation of the truths of scripture, tradition or preaching, not the source of truth (as in 1 above), but of power, witness and assurance. This concept of testimony is another legacy from the later stage of what had been the common teaching of Luther and Zwingli preserved in the Baptist movement. In it the more elitarian mysticism of a Denck becomes generally accessible. In view of the complementarity of these last two dimensions, the congregational (3) and the personal (4), we shall discuss their implications together in this section.

1. The concept of the Spirit in the free churches requires religious freedom. Within the general emphasis on the authority of the assembled community to take decisions (3), the stress lies on the illegitimacy of any restrictions imposed by an authority (or of course by a bishop). In the emphasis on personal appropriation (4) it is on the rejection of all compulsion in matters of faith. The argument was not at all obvious at the time; it was that faith was a result of the action of the Holy Spirit.[5] Whether 'faith' was understood in a more intellectual sense as acceptance of correct items of doctrine, or associated, in a more voluntaristic sense, with God's gracious word, both had to be regarded as spiritual gifts.

2. The local community's power of decision came to provide the basis for a degree of pluralism on the level of wider ecclesial unity. The communities cultivated unity between the various currents in the movement by means of mutual visits from their travelling apostles, correspondence and ad hoc synods. Major moments of unification such as Schlechtheim were regarded, as we have seen, as the action of the Spirit. Chroniclers and collectors of correspondence developed some common tradition, but the locally assembled community was never replaced or reduced in importance as the place of the Spirit's opus proprium.

3. Again following Luther and Zwingli, the Baptists regarded the

process of reconciling talk, which, with reference to Matt. 18:15ff, they called the 'rule of Christ', as one of the essential *notae ecclesiae*. What is described in Matt. 18:20 as the presence of Christ is called the Holy Spirit in the parallel passage John 20:22ff. This power of forgiveness, and in extreme cases of excommunication, was also not given to a specially selected priest but to the community (and in the positive case of reconciliation to every member).

4. The rejection of infant baptism does not just follow logically from the essential role of personal appropriation (4), but also from the binding nature of the rule of Christ. Only an adult can make a binding commitment to take part in the community's processes of discussion. The confession which is a prerequisite for the validity of baptism is also a work of the Spirit, and it therefore has no meaning to celebrate the form of such a confession in the case of a child without its content.[6]

For the rest the connections between the concept of the Spirit and individual points of specifically Baptist teaching are less direct. Where particular attitudes were controversial (the refusal to swear oaths, non-resistance), the debates did not turn on the Spirit. Where there was more common ground with the rest of the Zwinglians (the principle of scripture, eucharistic doctrine, criticism of 'ceremonies'), the appeal to the Spirit was similar to that of other reformed groups. After the disasters of Müntzer and Münster every temptation to primitive 'enthusiasm' was banned, and all imminent expectation was sobered. All that remained to be taken account of theologically was the painful journey of the remnants of the free church reformation, now generally persecuted. And the last action of the Spirit to be mentioned is the incorporation of the disciple into Christ's way of the cross which is hinted at in the eucharist: endurance under torture and exile.

> The moment came
> . . . and with great joy
> she leapt on to the wood.
> Of his free will
> God for her had contended.
> She now with fervour
> her soul into his hands commended:
> Let him send his Spirit
> and show her at the last
> his help and grace.[7]

Although the number of Baptists executed amounted to no more than a few thousand, perhaps fewer than the number killed in war in the same decades, the sense of being a community of martyrs following in the footsteps of Jesus remained a formative influence on the surviving Baptists.

Translated by Francis McDonagh

Notes

1. Heinold Fast *Der linke Flügel der Reformation (Klassiker des Protestantismus* IV) (Bremen 1962) pp. xxviiff. It is true that the sociology of religion is making a similar attempt to rehabilitate the term 'sect' and give it a value-free descriptive content. However, it remains questionable whether such an attempt at refinement can ever succeed on the basis of ecumenical linguistic pluralism.

2. Fritz Blanke *Brüder in Christo*, Zwingli-Bücherei 71 (Zurich 1955); see also his 'Täufertum und Reformation' in *Reformatio* (1957) pp. 212ff, reprinted in Blanke *Aus der Welt der Reformation* (Zurich 1960). The terminology now accepted in the ecumenical movement ('Baptists' instead of 'Anabaptists', 'free church' instead of 'sect') is partly the result of Blanke's work.

3. We give no source references for individual figures. Bibliographical details in Fast op. cit., biographical details in Hans-Jürgen Goertz *Radikale Reformatoren* (Schwarze Reihe 183) (Munich 1978).

4. Fast, op. cit.

5. The Baptists were by no means alone in this battle for religious freedom. Humanists and freethinkers (branded at the time as 'Epicureans' or 'Libertines'), and spiritualists (2. 2 above) had similar interests and used similar arguments.

6. As Rollin S. Armour describes in *Anabaptist Baptism*, the various Baptist thinkers of the early period, though differing in language and reasoning, all started from the premise that an ontic change produced by the Spirit took place in the candidate before the administration of water baptism and not as a result of it.

7. From verses 31 and 32 of Hymn 17 in the Baptist collection *Auss Bundt*, on the execution of Maria Beckum on November 13 1544, in Delden (Twente/Oberijssel).

Alexandre Ganoczy

Word and Spirit in the Catholic Tradition

SHOULD WE wish to attempt a Catholic approach towards the problems that goaded Luther, Zwingli and Calvin into a harsh debate with the
Spiritualists and Anabaptists of their day, then we shall find an avenue of
approach, embracing both criticism and self-criticism, ready to hand in
the history of doctrine. For there must be sound historical reasons for the
surprisingly small amount of space devoted in the doctrinal pronouncements of Trent to the theological relationship of Word and Spirit
and to the significance of this relationship for the existence of the Church.

Now the Reformation provoked the emergence of the Catholic Church
in the confessional sense of the word. But was this Church at that time in
any position to shed light on the relation between God's Word and Spirit
with dual reference to the demands of theology and real life? What sort of
hermeneutics and pneumatology stood at the disposal of the Roman
teaching office in terms of its own tradition? Was it actually necessary for
a good four hundred years to elapse before the materialisation of a
biblically grounded and ecclesiologically integrated doctrine of Revelation and the Holy Spirit, an ecumenically significant example of which
was furnished by the Second Vatican Council? And of what provenance
were the impulses and ingredients that brought about such a development, or renewal, of doctrine? Did they hail exclusively from the Catholic
side, or perhaps also from that of the Reformation? It was at any rate the
latter which was the more severely confronted with the problem of
'Enthusiasm'. The question is therefore appropriate, whether one of the
Reformers was not perhaps best placed to do some justice to the concerns
of the so-called 'Enthusiasts', concerns the legitimacy of which was
rooted in the Gospel itself. This question is endowed at the present day

48

with a further dimension over and above that of its historical and ecumenical significance. For are not men once more looking, at this precise point of time, for experience of God and the Spirit both inside *and* outside the 'Word'?

1. AN UNDERDEVELOPED PNEUMATOLOGY

As we review the most important pronouncements issued on the subject of the Holy Spirit by the teaching office in the first fifteen centuries of western Christendom, we are struck by a considerable dearth of ideas *vis-à-vis* the New Testament data.[1] The doctrine of the ('immanent') Trinity is almost the sole context in which the Holy Spirit is spoken of. Pneumatology is almost completely exhausted in the definition of the unity of essence and of the relationships of distinction, procession and mission that obtain between the three divine Persons (see DS 526f., 800-806). Apart from a list of the 'seven gifts of the Spirit' (DS 178; cf. 183), the pronouncements of the teaching office do not address themselves in any detail to the role of the Spirit in the economy of salvation; a matter which is dwelt on by Paul in the context of congregational life, by Luke in that of mission, and by John in that of the personal act of faith. At this point our critical formulation of the question appears justified. For had not the western Church, especially in the mediaeval period, simply become too little marked by joy in its proclamation and in its charismas, and had it not become too little stamped by the missionary urge to be able to enter fully upon its Pauline and Lucan heritage? And was it not too little oriented towards the requirement of individuals for experience of God to be able to accord even Johannine pneumatology its native rights? The objection can scarcely be raised that the teaching office, as an organ chiefly designed to furnish dogmatic safeguards, would have had no responsibility for such constructive work. For the various 'spiritualisms' of Cathari, Albegensians and Waldensians could, precisely be means of the challenges they posed, have had a theologically fruitful effect; just as the Corinthian 'proto-gnosis' and the gnosis of the ancient Church had prompted Paul and John in turn to develop a carefully balanced doctrine of the Spirit. Furthermore, the Roman teaching office could have turned its 'eastern contacts' to better effect, in order to overcome this chronic state of pneumatological underdevelopment!

The teaching office articulated the relationship between the divine Word and Spirit principally by means of the *doctrine of inspiration*. It seems to interpret the credal statement (initially of eastern provenance), that the Holy Spirit spoke through the Prophets—as also through the Law and the Apostles (DS 46, 48)—purely in the sense of a *statement with reference to the past*. Thus it is taught that the books of the Old and New

Testaments were written 'in virtue of the inspiration of one and the same Holy Spirit' (DS 1334). There is no corresponding statement with reference to the present appended, say, to the credal statement (of exclusively eastern provenance) about the Holy Spirit as 'Giver of life' (DS 42, 62, 71) and as 'Paraclete' (DS 41, 44, 60). Such a course of action would have made evident the persisting, current and continually new work of the Holy Spirit in the hearts of those who seek to hear the Word of God in the here and now of their believing existence. At this place too the deficiencies of the doctrinal tradition of the western Middle Ages make themselves felt, a factor that may well shed some light on the embarrassment that it felt when confronted, for example, with the mysticism of a Meister Eckhart and, prior to that, with the theology of love of a P. G. Olivi.[2] We are tempted to ask whether the Reformation did not *have to* come, not only to make good the pneumatological deficit to which we have referred, but also to cope with the spiritual hunger experienced by many believers.

2. A REFORMATION CONTRIBUTION: CALVIN

The sixteenth-century movements of Spiritualists and Baptists have been aptly dubbed a *radical outbidding* of Reformation Christianity.[3] The first of these groups (including Karlstadt, Müntzer, Denk and Franck) aspired to an *immediacy* in the soul's relationship to God which exceeded the bounds of what Luther had taught. The upshot of this was a marked relativisation not only of the institutional Church but also of the Bible, in favour of the present operation of the Spirit. As Müntzer robustly warned, without the 'living testimony of God', that is, the activity of the Holy Spirit in the reader, the latter *experiences* nothing of the reality of God, 'even if he should have devoured a hundred thousand Bibles'.[4] Denk went still further, and for him the biblical reports had no other function beyond simply serving as an 'illustration of the spiritual path of salvation'[5] for the subject enlightened by the Spirit. The Baptists, on the other hand, were far less disposed to call the scriptural principle of the Reformation into question. Indeed, one of their basic demands consisted in the *unrestricted observance* of the biblical directives, in order to render possible the emergence of a true Church of the 'pure'. This was intended to be a genuine fellowship of believing men, who pledged themselves to holy and austere conduct by means of the freely and deliberately performed baptism of the Spirit.[6]

Thus we are confronted on the one hand with the strictest biblicism and on the other with a radical 'actualism' of the Spirit; and it was between these two extremes that the Reformers Luther, Zwingli and Calvin saw themselves impelled to cleave unreservedly to the correct, 'evangelical' path. By this they understood a path of salvation which embraced the

Word-Spirit relationship in such a way that neither the religious subject's experiential requirements (even the Reformers drew partly on the heritage of late mediaeval mysticism!) nor the communal structures of the Church should come to grief. In this endeavour Jean Calvin attained a synthesis which is particularly remarkable from the point of view of the Catholic tradition.

How did Calvin tackle the unity in tension of Word and Spirit? In what did he locate the criterion whereby the correct relationship between the two forms of appearance of the one God might be discerned? The answer is to be found in a consistently maintained *Christocentrism* conceived as a hermeneutical principle of the Christian existence in faith. It was doubtless Luther's merit to have renewed the Christocentric thought of Pauline theology with prophetic force. Nevertheless, Calvin's systematic approach was apparently still required to elevate the notion of relationship to the Lord (Kyrios) in the sense of 1 Cor. 12:3, along with its application to the upbuilding of the Church (see 1 Cor. 14), in a stroke of hermeneutical foresight to the status of criterion in the 'discerning of the spirits' which was urgently necessary at that time.

Calvin had a systematic pneumatology which he owed to his own ingenuity. According to his scheme, the Holy Spirit was no longer a hovering, ambiguous entity which could be interpreted in an arbitrary manner, but He was essentially the *Spirit of Christ as the Logos of God for men*. Not only does this give us the great interpretative principle for the contemporary debate with the 'radicals'; it also creates a foundation for a synthetic understanding of faith in the sense of a substantial and indeed supra-confessional Catholicity.[7]

Calvin's Christocentric hermeneutics hold fast when examined in three specific areas which are essentially concerned with the operation of the Spirit. These are bible reading, the eucharist and synodal bodies.

1. *The Spirit of Christ and Bible reading*

It is not sufficient, when dealing with the question of *bible reading,* simply to recall the inspiration of the Bible. The reader must himself be opened up by the power of the present 'secret testimony of the Holy Spirit';[8] for the will of the Spirit is to give 'inward instruction' to the reader.[9] When correctly understood, this takes place in such a way that, first of all, the believer expects nothing from the Spirit of Christ which the latter cannot bring. 'The office of the Spirit promised to us (by Christ!) does not consist in fabricating new and unheard-of revelations, . . . but his office is precisely to seal in us the doctrine that is put into our hearts in the Gospel'.[10] There is a distincly anti-enthusiastic cutting edge about these remarks; but even so the context demonstrates a certain understanding on Calvin's part for his opponents' fundamental concern. 'The letter therefore is dead, and the law of the Lord (!) kills its readers when it is severed from the grace of Christ and only perceived by the ears . . . But if it is effectually impressed on our hearts by the Spirit, *if it exhibits Christ,* it is the word of life converting the soul'.[11] As a matter of fact, the Spirit of Christ can show Christ alone, as the 'scopus' and centre of the entire Scripture, to each individual only when he hears, reads and meditates on the Word in a state of 'preparedness for Christ'. Christ is the Word and Christ's the Spirit; so how could Word and Spirit possibly contradict one another? This notion also holds true with reference to the Word of God attested in Scripture. For there too the Lord 'has firmly and *mutually* bound together the certainty of his Word and his Spirit'.[12] The biblical Word reveals the Spirit of God and of Christ; the Spirit of God and of Christ illuminates the biblical Word. Word and Spirit form no contradiction, for they are correlative to each other and are meant to be used as such.

2. *The Spirit of Christ and the Eucharist*

Now unless this thesis finds parallels in Calvin's understanding of the *sacraments* and the congregation, it would scarcely accord with the tradition of the universal Church in general or with the Pauline tradition in particular (see 2 Cor. 3:6, 14-18). But precisely this is the case, for a similar service of *mediation* falls to the share of the Spirit of Christ in the eucharist too. In the eucharist he no longer simply unites human words with the eternal and living Word of God; rather, he here unites the outward forms of bread and wine with the exalted Lord who, in virtue of his exaltation, is forever ready to sacrifice himself. 'We say that Christ descends to us *both* in the outward symbol *and also* in his Spirit, in order that he may truly make our souls alive with the substance of his flesh and blood.'[13] Certainly the work of the Spirit is not exhausted in some kind of 'transfinalisation' of the elements. Its range extends further to the eucharistic guests themselves; in the sacramental Word-act they are 'illuminated' and 'opened', in order that, believing in what takes place here, they may receive it as God's Word and deed.[14]

3. *The Spirit of Christ and the Congregation*

Lastly, this correlation of Word and Spirit is exhibited also in various extra-sacramental aspects of *congregational life.* Calvin has a rather richly developed doctrine of 'charisma', thought out in ecclesiological terms and built largely on Eph. 4:11-13; and he has a doctrine on the ecclesiastical office, according to which the servants of the Word are described, in the sense of 1 Cor. 3:5-9, as fellow workers with God through the Holy Spirit and thought of as committed to a collegiality commensurate with this calling.[15] Here too the Pneuma mediates between Christ and his con-

gregation, between the divine Word and everything human. One cul-
mination of this practical pneumatology surely lies in the enforcements of
Synods and Councils. When they assemble in the name of Christ and are
instructed by his Spirit, Councils of the universal Church are qualified to
form dogmas and Synods of local churches to achieve a proper formulation and interpretation of the creed.[16]

The French Reformer sees the Christocentric correlation of Word and
Spirit at work in each of these areas: bible reading, the eucharist and
congregational life. Through this vision he recovers a goodly portion of
Pauline and Johannine pneumatology, so that their Lucan counterpart,
with its missionary slant, remains the only major New Testament model
to which he pays scant attention. Should these findings stand up to
scrutiny, then Calvin might be regarded as a representative of at least a
'substantial Catholicity', and consequently as one who endeavoured to
grasp the *diversity* of the Spirit's spheres of operation in their complementary *unity*.[17] In this way he made a remarkable contribution, at
least on the theological level, towards overcoming the doubts entertained
by the enthusiasts, while at the same time displaying some understanding
for their root concern. Was not a similar achievement to be expected from
the Council of Trent?

3. STIRRINGS OF PNEUMATOLOGICAL DEVELOPMENT AT THE COUNCIL OF TRENT

1. *Spirit and Council*

The Fathers of Trent were in agreement with Calvin on one matter,
namely in their conviction that a genuinely Christian *Assembly of the
Church* can only be one which has 'come together in the Holy Spirit' (DS
1501) and which, working under his 'presidency' (DS 1667) and 'guidance' (DS 1635), allows him to 'instruct' it (see also DS 1726, 1738). It
may be regretted, however, that these fundamental theological insights
only crop up in the Tridentine texts as stereotyped formulas, largely in the
form of introductions to decrees. They do not lead into any kind of
hermeneutical reflection on the subject, say, on the relationship between
the 'Word of God' and the 'word of the Church'.

2. *The Spirit and Justification*

The pneumatological balance-sheet shows up a much larger credit
when we turn to the doctrines of *justification* and the sacraments. We
notice first of all how the doctrinal decision '*De iustificatione*' moves in
the very territory where both the Reformation theory of Word and faith
and the Anabaptists' desire for mature faith-commitment are likewise at
home: the beginning and completion of justification in *adults* (DS 1525).

The Council Fathers speak of a 'call' issued by God's 'prevenient grace', and accordingly of a thoroughly verbal utterance on the part of God in Christ, which invites all men to a conversion undergone freely, consciously and maturely. In this way, 'by means of his awakening and assisting grace they are prepared to apply themselves to their own justification, in free consent to and *co-operation* with this grace. In this contact, where God affects the heart of man through the light of the *Holy Spirit,* on the one hand man does not remain entirely passive . . ., while on the other he cannot, on the strength of his free will without the grace of God, raise himself to righteousness before him' (ibid.). In the third thesis appended to this doctrinal statement there even ensues a sharpened expression of the Fathers' meaning couched in genuinely pneumatological terms: 'Without the prevenient inspiration and assistance of the *Holy Spirit*', man cannot 'believe, hope, love and repent as is necessary for him to participate in the grace of justification' (DS 1553). Here, presumably by recourse to the late mediaeval identification of Spirit with 'caritas' (see DS 1530, 1561) or '*gratia increata*', the same 'prevenience' is ascribed to the Holy Spirit as is attributed to God's gracious call of invitation. Therefore what God does to man, he does simultaneously by means of his Word and his Spirit. Even if not couched in such expressly Christological terms, the Tridentine formula is similar to that of Calvin. The cause of the difference between the two lies in the diversity of their respective starting-points. Calvin proceeds from Christ as the Logos of God, the Council of Trent from God in His eternal salvific will.

Now it is remarkable how our quotations from Trent suggest a positive evaluation of human *freedom* by their use of the catchword 'cooperari'. When God's Word issues its call, it does not cast a hypnotic spell on the one who is called, for he can reject it. The prevenient Spirit works fundamentally as an offer of help which intends to compel no one. But a free consent to and a free co-operation with grace only becomes a possibility in virtue of this offer. Calvin would certainly not have gone as far as this; the furthest he went in this direction was to label church office-holders in the performance of their duties as 'fellow-workers with God' on the basis of 1 Cor. 3:5-9.[18] The question whether certain Anabaptists, with their pretension to achieve the highest degree of moral strictness, would not have shown more understanding for the synergistic doctrine of Trent, would merit a detailed investigation. The Baptists of Zürich and the Netherlands, not to mention their fanatical comrades in Münster, were hardly predisposed towards quietism!

In this context of synergism it is worth noting the consistency with which the Council regards sin, in accordance with Eph. 4:30, as 'grieving the Holy Spirit' (DS 1543, 1630, 1699). This teaching surely moves on the same plane as that on the freedom of choice which we have already stressed above, which is not entirely unrelated to the Anabaptist quest for a *personally accountable* faith-commitment.

3. *Spirit and Sacrament*

No particular emphasis need be laid on the fact that, in the doctrinal decisions on the *sacraments* too, the operation of the Pneuma—as prevenient, justifying, sanctifying, changing, enabling and perfecting—is rendered explicit in a similar fashion. The Tridentine doctrine of the Eucharist is different from Calvin's, though, in that it makes scarcely any mention of pneumatology. For example, there is not a word on the epiclesis, nor is there any allusion to the present operation of the Holy Spirit as possessing constitutive significance for the sacrament. Was this silence simply determined by apologetic considerations?[19]

4. *Spirit, Scripture and Church*

But when we turn to the only text which deals *ex professo* with the doctrine of *Holy Scripture,* the result of our investigations is thoroughly disappointing. First of all, no attempt is made to undergrid this doctrine in terms of the theology of revelation or of Christology. Hence there is no fundamental theology of the divine Word. When Jesus is called the Christ, the sense is not that he is the self-revelation of God in person, nor that he is purely and simply the revealer. The title 'Son of God' is mentioned only once and then in apposition; and Christ makes but one appearance in almost 'Jesuological' shorthand as the one who 'proclaimed' the Gospel 'with his own mouth' and gave it to his apostles to preach (DS 1501). This then is another statement oriented to the past, similar to that about the inspiration of the sacred books by the Holy Spirit which took place at one particular point of time (see DS 1334). This Gospel is indeed termed the 'source of all salvation-bringing truth and moral order'; but in the next sentence this seems to be forgotten once more, at least if it is to be understood in the sense of a presently flowing stream. The Council contents itself with the statement that 'this truth and order [is] *contained* both in written books *and* (!) in unwritten traditions', being designed to be handed on like an inheritance (DS 1501).

The idea expressed here is of an almost symmetrical *juxtaposition* of Bible traditions, ('which the apostles received from the mouth of Christ or which, by the inspiration of the Holy Spirit, were handed down as it were from hand to hand from the apostles themselves'); but it makes no contribution at all to the task of clarifying the concept of revelation. Such clarification is achieved all the less in that the Council Fathers in all probability made Bible and traditions the object of an 'equal piety and veneration' (DS 1501). There is no mention of a criterion for ascertaining precisely what is to be understood by such highly venerable traditions.

This oversight implicitly opens the door to the risk of an unclear or arbitrary understanding of the Gospel; but this danger is countered by the device of placing at least the *interpretation of Scripture* in the hands of 'Holy Mother Church' (*de facto* the teaching office). 'In matters of faith and morals no one shall presume . . . in reliance on his own cleverness to twist Holy Scripture according to a sense which is contrary to that which the . . . Church held and holds. It is her right to judge the true sense and the explanation of the Holy Scriptures' (DS 1507).

From the dogmatic point of view, this attitude held good in the ensuing period; and even today no Catholic theologian would quibble with the substance of it. But it may be doubted whether, either then or later, this principle was in any position to answer the question which, produced by what may be termed a famine of personal experience of God, arose with Luther's and Calvin's theology of revelation and with the radicalism of the enthusiasts. It is indeed the case that even in the province of piety a phenomenal Catholic Reformation was achieved in the wake of the Council; but by and large this Reformation was nourished from sources other than a scriptural theology of Word and Spirit.

4. THE DEVELOPMENT OF PNEUMATOLOGY AT THE SECOND VATICAN COUNCIL

Would it be highly presumptuous to maintain that the seminal insights of Calvin and of Trent[20] were first developed in the sense of a higher 'substantial Catholicity' at the Second Vatican Council? Let this question remain open for the moment, and let us merely establish the following points.

The most recent Council, in its treatment of a 'Christocentric theology of revelation', adopts a position squarely based on the New Testament. Revelation is once more essentially the *self-revelation* of God, whose truth 'enlightens [us] in Christ, who is at once the mediator and the fullness of all revelation'.[21] This is no longer a statement referring only to the past. In the ensuing statements too, which take up, among others, the Johannine understanding of revelation, the temporal scope of the Conciliar pronouncements remains by and large directed towards the *present*. The same can likewise be said of the seminal ideas of Pauline pneumatology that are worked into the documents. The 'obedience of faith' (Rom. 16:26) cannot be performed 'without (see Calvin!) the inner assistance of the Holy Spirit, who must move the heart and turn it to God, and open the eyes of the understanding (DV 5). Statements such as this are well placed to do justice to the viewpoint of the religious subject in his actual search for an experience of God to help him on his forward way, as was already the case with Calvin and in the Tridentine doctrine of conversion. As a matter of fact, for all its adherence to the classical doctrine of inspiration (see DV 7, 9, 11/1, 13/2), with Vatican II the conviction is coming into vogue that the Word-related operation of the Spirit is not exhausted in his once for all activity on the authors and the text of the Holy Scriptures, but that it is continued in his persistent activity on the hearts of those who hear and read the Word of God attested in Scripture. The consequences of this development are not restricted simply to the spiritual needs of the individual. On the contrary, it results in a many-sided teamwork in the Church's task of *ascertaining the truth*. 'With the assistance of the Holy Spirit, the apostolic tradition knows progress in the Church. The understanding of the things and words handed on grows *by means of the meditation and study of believers* which they think through in their hearts (see Luke 2:19, 51)' (DV 8/3).[22] There is further allusion in the documents to this convergence of the seekers after truth, in which quest the 'spiritual experience' of believers is said to have its proper part, along with the proclamatory work of the bishops.

Towards the close of the document this train of thought even attains a genuinely *missionary* perspective roughly commensurate with Lucan pneumatology. It is 'the Holy Spirit through whom the living voice of the Gospel resounds in the Church and, via the Church, in the world' (DV 8/4). In other places too the Second Vatican Council is marked by a consciousness of mission resolutely directed towards the world, of a kind for which one seeks in vain in the Reformers or in Trent. With this consciousness a real primitive Christian Exodus-dynamic is flowing into the ecclesial landscape—always a welcome thing, whether it is a question of overcoming enthusiastic subjectivism or of institutional rigidity. The missionary characteristic of going beyond oneself was always at once a fruit of the Spirit and an active hearing of the Word!

It is certainly true that the Second Vatican Council does not think out this apostolic dynamic of the word of proclamation independently of its doctrine—to which it accords excessive emphasis—of the *teaching office* of pope, Council and bishops (DV 7/1, 9/1, 10/1 etc.). Even so, ecumenically disposed readers may well take pleasure in one pronouncement, namely that 'The teaching office is not above the Word of God but *serves* it by teaching nothing but what has been handed down, because it *hears* the Word of God in complete reverence on divine instruction and with the assistance of the Holy Spirit' (DV 10/2). This statement once more brings Calvin to mind, for he was wont to term the Church in its learning function as 'sobria discipula',[23] as a teacher of the Gospel herself willing to learn.

In the opinion of many commentators, however, a weak point of the Council remains the still unsatisfactory clarification it gives of the relationship between *Scripture and Tradition*. The unhappily formulated Tridentine 'two-source' theory was indeed dropped, and the concept of tradition was understood rather as a function of handing on entrusted to the successors of the Apostles than as a sum of truths of revelation additional to Scripture.[24] Nevertheless the specific function of Scripture is not expressed in a way that might remove the scales of misunderstanding once and for all from the eyes of the Protestant observer.

5. EN ROUTE TO A 'MORE CATHOLIC' UNDERSTANDING OF WORD AND SPIRIT

A Catholic understanding of Word and Spirit? The doctrine of the Second Vatican Council here outlined might well be called 'more Catholic' than that which was hitherto deemed to be 'Catholic'. This is the case when we do not simply have confessional Catholicity in mind, but also a 'substantial Catholicity' which consists in fidelity to the many aspects of revelation in their constitutive convergence and unity. Especially when we read this teaching on divine revelation in the context of the other Conciliar documents, its proximity to the riches of the New Testament pneumatologies becomes apparent. For then the relationship of Word and Spirit appears within the framework of a Church which understands itself as a charismatically structured, eschatologically moved, apostolically active, synodically governed, sacramentally articulated and mystically inspired community of believing men. Such an understanding of the being of the Church corresponds to a pneumatology which draws on the understanding of the Spirit evidenced both by the great Old Testament prophets and by Paul, Luke and John; and it may therefore be termed *increasingly* substantial-Catholic. But whether it is in a position to cope any better with today's hunger for a personal experience of God than did the confessional Churches of the Reformation in face of the fundamental concern of the 'enthusiasts' (to the extent that this concern contained genuinely Christian elements), the future alone can tell.

Notes

1. This impression is gained by a glance at the indexes of Denzinger-Schönmetzer (1963 ed.) pp. 812, 816-821, 832, 840 and of Neuner-Roos *Der Glaube der Kirche* (1971 ed.) p. 574.

2. See V. Heynck 'Olivi' LThK 7, pp. 1149ff.

3. Thus B. Moeller 'Die radikale Reformation: Spiritualisten und Täufer' in R. Kottje & B. Moeller (ed.) *Ökumenische Kirchengeschichte* vol. 2 (Mainz 1978) pp. 334-342.

4. Ibid. p. 336.

5. Ibid. p. 337.

6. See ibid. pp. 338-342.

7. See esp. W. Krusche *Das Wirken des Heiligen Geistes nach Calvin* (Göttingen 1957).

8. *Institutio* 1.7.4.

9. Ibid. 1.7.5.

10. Ibid. 1.9.1.

11. Ibid. 1.9.3.

12. Ibid.

13. Ibid. IV.17.24.

14. See ibid. IV.14.8f.

15. See A. Ganoczy *Ecclesia ministrans. Dienende Kirche und kirchlicher Dienst nach Calvin* (Freiburg-Basel-Wien 1968) pp. 178-195.

16. See ibid. pp. 56f., 227, 266, 282, 302.

17. On Calvin's 'Catholicity' see A. Ganoczy's foreword to H. Scholl *Calvinus catholicus* (Freiburg-Basel-Wien 1974) pp. 5-8.

18. See *Calvini Opera* (Corpus Reformatorum) 49, pp. 348-352.

19. On Baptism see DS 1514, 1524, 1615; on Penance 1670, 1678 (a remarkably pneumatological account of 'attritio'), 1684; on Unction of the sick 1696, 1699; on Ordination 1768, 1774.

20. It is questionable whether Calvin and the Council of Trent are comparable 'loci theologici'. It goes without saying that the importance of an individual theologian is different in kind from that of an Ecumenical Council. Thus it would certainly be more appropriate in this context to confront the Council of Trent with a number of Reformed confessions and catechisms. It is principally the *synthetic* character striven after by both Calvin and Trent that has enabled us to attempt the present comparison between them in order to furnish an answer to a definite challenge on the part of the Reformation with joint reference to God's Word and Spirit.

21. Dogmatic Constitution on Divine Revelation *Dei Verbum,* hereafter referred to in the text by the abbreviation DV, p. 2.

22. The aspect of 'study' receives further treatment below (e.g., DV 12/2, 22/1) in the context of exegetical research and the continual need to improve upon translations of the Bible.

23. *Institutio* (1536 ed.) ch. 6 Calvini Opera (CR) 1, p. 215.

24. See J. Ratzinger's commentary on DV 7/2 and 9 LThK-K II pp. 517, 523-526.

Part III

Office and Spirit:
The Question of Rome

Battista Mondin

The Holy Spirit as Legitimation of the Papacy

'THE HOLY SPIRIT IS A GREAT UNKNOWN.' This phrase, readily and frequently repeated by preachers, was true up to a few years ago; today it is no longer so. The Church has recently become aware of the reality of the Holy Spirit, feeling him close and calling him by name, appealing to him, loving him, praising him, and seeking to move under his sure and stimulating influence. It is almost as though we had finally entered the prophetic age of the Spirit foretold by Gioachino da Fiore.

This rediscovery of the Holy Spirit has had a profound effect, not only on the *praxis* of the Church and of individual Christians, but also on theological reflection. The events of salvation history and the Christian message are now interpreted in terms of the *pneuma* or Spirit, aquiring in this way a profounder, more vital spiritual sense.

This interpretation of the Word of God in terms of the Spirit proves extraordinarily rich and fruitful, especially for ecclesiology, both in general and in the treatment of its individual aspects, including that which relates to the papacy.

1. SETTING OUT THE THEME

1. *The attitude of the post-tridentine Church*

It is well known that in the post-tridentine period, because of the polemical reaction provoked by the strongly Spirit-based ecclesiology of the Reformers, Catholic theologians developed their doctrine of the Church along markedly juridical, institutional and social lines, ignoring the spiritual, interior, 'pneumatic' dimension, which was considered irrelevant as far as providing a correct definition of the Church was

63

concerned. As a result their interest was concentrated on the visible, external, institutional and social aspects of the community founded by Jesus Christ. In such a perspective, respect for the papacy, as the key institution of the Catholic Church, naturally increased, and the growth of theological reflection in this direction reached its climax in the definition of papal infallibility proclaimed by Vatican I and confirmed a century later by Vatican II.

2. *Arguments for the papacy*

In a legalistic and socially-orientated ecclesiology, the arguments adduced in support of the papacy were of three kinds: *biblical, historical and sociological.* In the first place those texts were gathered together in which Jesus places Peter at the head of the apostolic college, conferring on him special powers of leadership and assuring him of the extraordinary assistance of the Holy Spirit. Then it was shown, on the basis of historical research, that the authority of Peter was passed on to the Bishop of Rome and that the exercise of this authority by the Sovereign Pontiff was adapted progressively to the wants of the age and the needs of the Church. Finally, the biblical witness and the historical tradition of the Church were strengthened by rational arguments brought forward to demonstrate that it is of the essence of every perfect society to structure itself hierarchically and to entrust to a single person the government of all its members.

Towards the middle of the twentieth century, in the climate created by *Mystici Corporis* and as a result of the renewal which was causing a profound upheaval in all areas of Catholic thinking, ecclesiology too underwent a substantial transformation: by degrees it abandoned the juridico-social perspective for a perspective that is sacramental, orientated towards communion and the Spirit. The 'Age of the Spirit' has not yet dawned, but theology is already favourably disposed to the entry of the Spirit; indeed, the arguments now put forward in support of the papacy frequently appeal to the third person of the Trinity. Here, however, the question immediately arises: in the present theological and cultural climate, which is so very different from that which preceded it, is the doctrine of the papacy, which, as we have seen, was elaborated predominantly on a juridical basis and for polemical purposes, still capable of presenting valid arguments in support of such a structure, and above all arguments derived from the spiritual aspect of the Church? What follows is intended as an answer to this challenging question.

3. *Two fundamental aspects of the Church*

First and foremost, let us recognise that the Church is a complex and mysterious reality, to all intents and purposes ineffable. It is possible

neither to define it adequately nor to achieve any exhaustive understanding of it. All one can do is to try and elucidate some of its aspects
and, by considering it from various points of view through a careful and
deep examination of its many aspects, by degrees to come closer to some
kind of fuller understanding of the mystery of the Church.

Today it is a self-evident and universally-recognised fact that the
Church, as the mystical body of Christ, possesses two aspects that are
fundamental to it—its *corporeal and visible* aspect and its *'pneumatic' and
invisible* aspect. And for this reason no exhaustive study of the Church
can afford to ignore either of them. And this applies to all the organs of
which the mystical body is composed, including the papacy. A full understanding and justification of that particular body requires that the latter
be studied from the sacramental, mystical and 'pneumatic' point of view,
and not only from the juridical and social point of view. Given the scope
of the present article, the primary purpose of which is to describe the
reality of the papacy from the 'pneumatic' point of view, that is the
perspective within which I will situate what I have to say, without however forgetting that one must take it in conjunction with the other if one
wants to acquire a right understanding of its effective reality.

4. *Two ways of looking at the papacy*

The papacy can be considered in two ways: as an historical institution
or as a living reality in the present exercise of its functions. Consequently
the Holy Spirit can be invoked in support of the papacy in two different
ways. If one looks on the papacy as an historical institution, one invokes
the Holy Spirit to affirm that the papacy has a *divine, supernatural* origin.
If on the other hand, one considers it as a living reality in the exercise of its
functions, one will have recourse to the Holy Spirit in order to show that,
in the carrying out of certain activities at least, it enjoys a special form of
assistance from the Holy Spirit. Since the papacy, as far as the Catholic
faith is concerned, forms part of the essential structure of the Church, the
'pneumatic justification' is valid and indispensable in both cases. The
space I have at my disposal here does not allow me to treat adequately of
both aspects, and as far as the papacy as an historical institution is
concerned, a few brief references will have to suffice. On the other hand,
my treatment of the papacy as a living reality in the present exercise of its
functions will be fuller and carried out in greater depth.

2. THE PAPACY AS AN INSTITUTION WILLED BY THE HOLY SPIRIT

The Holy Spirit guided Jesus in the choice of the twelve and in the
appointment of Peter as their head (Luke 6:12ff.; Matt. 16:16ff.; John

21:15ff.). To the apostolic college and to Peter in particular, Jesus promised the assistance of the Holy Spirit: 'These things I have spoken to you, while I am still with you. But the Counsellor, the Holy Spirit, whom the Father will send in my name, he will teach you all things, and bring to your remembrance all that I have said to you' (John 14:25-26). 'When the Spirit of truth comes, he will guide you into all the truth; for he will not speak on his own authority, but whatever he hears he will speak, and he will declare to you the things that are to come' (John 16:13-14).

As these texts indicate, the assistance promised by Jesus to Peter and the other apostles relates to two things: (*a*) a better understanding of the truth announced by Jesus—a truth which during his earthly life was scarcely glimpsed by the disciples and barely understood at all; (*b*) the faithful preservation, with the memory of infallibility, of the doctrine of Jesus.

The promises made by Jesus were realised on the occasion of Pentecost. On that memorable day, while Peter, the apostles and the mother of Jesus, together with a number of pious women, 'were all together in one place [the cenacle]. And suddenly a sound came from heaven like the rush of a mighty wind, and it filled the house where they were sitting. And there appeared to them tongues as of fire, distributed and resting on each of them. And they were all filled with the Holy Spirit and began to speak in other tongues, as the Spirit gave them utterance' (Acts 2:2-4).

On the day of Pentecost, the Holy Spirit gave life to the Church and moulded it according to the basic pattern that had already been established by Jesus himself: disciples, apostles, Peter. This structural pattern endured throughout the apostolic period and is clearly recognisable at the Council of Jerusalem, even though, in the same period, new hierarchical grades (presbyters and deacons), which did not feature in the community founded by Jesus, were beginning to emerge. It is unthinkable that such a structural pattern, precisely because willed by the Holy Spirit, should be reserved exclusively to the apostolic age, and it must be regarded as destined to continue into later ages. In fact it did last even after the death of Peter, into the post-apostolic period, while the roles proper to the individual grades of the hierarchy gradually became crystallised. The successors of Peter in the see of Rome were increasingly openly recognised as having a special position and charism, and this not as a result of bargaining or arrogance, but on the strength of that communion of charity which the Holy Spirit diffuses into the hearts of Christ's followers according to a determined hierarchical order.

That the role of the papacy grew progressively more powerful thanks to the Holy Spirit and not to human astuteness seems obvious to anyone who believes that not only is the birth of the Church (and the birth of Jesus himself) the work of the Holy Spirit, but so is its development, at least in so far as important and decisive moments and aspects (such as the papacy) are concerned.

3. THE PRESENT EXERCISE OF PAPAL AUTHORITY TAKES PLACE THROUGH THE POWER OF THE SPIRIT

It is possible to justify the papacy on the basis of the Holy Spirit not only along diachronic (historical) lines, but also along synchronic (structural) lines, by examining the essential components of the Church as they exist and receive concrete expression at the present moment.

1. *Structural and 'pneumatic' elements*

(*a*) As in the past, so too today, the Church has two fundamental aspects, the *structural* or visible and the *'pneumatic'* or invisible. The first fulfils the role of body, the second that of soul.

(*b*) The basic principle of the structural aspect is the institution, or rather the *hierarchy* with all its grades (including that of the laity!) The first principle of the inner aspect is the Holy Spirit.

(*c*) The two are intimately connected, each penetrating the other at a profound level, in a manner analogous to the union and compenetration which exists between the human body and soul. The 'pneumatic' aspect, therefore, is neither objectified nor manifested without the structural; just as the structural, in its turn, is neither objectified nor operative without the spiritual.

(*d*) The Church has an organic structure, or rather a structure composed of many elements, each of which has a distinct role and a particular function to fulfil. It is not like a heap of sand or an ocean of water, in which the grains or drops are all equivalent and can occupy, indifferently, any position whatever. And in addition, besides being organic the structure of the Church is also hierarchical: there are within it bodies which exercise functions of service, assistance and guidance with respect to others. Such, in the Catholic Church, are the papacy, the episcopate and the presbyterate.

(*e*) These hierarchical bodies have been *willed and established by the Holy Spirit,* as Scripture and Tradition explicitly bear witness. On the basis of such testimony the Council of Trent declared: 'If anyone maintains that in the Catholic Church there is no hierarchy, instituted by divine ordinance and composed of bishops, priests and ministers, let him be anathema' (Session XXIII, can. 6).

(*f*) Corresponding to every structural element there is a 'pneumatic' element, a *charism* which makes it operative. So, even if there are in the Church 'independent' charisms—charisms, that is, which are not linked to any of the official ministries—they do not set themselves up against the hierarchy as the principle which gives the Church its structure. Christ, in fact, through the action of the Holy Spirit, builds up his body by means of a plurality of ministries, which the Spirit in fact brings to birth within it in order to make it fit to fulfil its role. Charisms and ministries interpenetrate one another and mutually enfold one another: there is no ministry, even the most official that is not also a gift of the Spirit, and there is no charism that is not also a service of the community.

(g) In the Catholic Church the *papacy* is one of the *essential structural elements*. Gathering together the heritage of a two-thousand-year-old tradition, Vatican II proposed once again to the faithful that they should firmly believe the 'teaching about the institution, the perpetuity, the force and reason for the sacred primacy of the Roman Pontiff and of his infallible teaching authority' (*Lumen Gentium* III, 18).

2. *Functional and charismatic elements*

(h) The Pope is a pastor, singled out from among pastors for the purpose of safeguarding and increasing the unity of the ecclesial communion. As Bishop of Rome he belongs to the body of bishops. In relation to that body, therefore, and indeed in relation to the entire ecclesial community, he exercises the function of head, teacher and guide.

(i) This function (of head, teacher and guide) belong to the charismatic and *not to the purely sociological* order, in that it is exercised in the power of the Holy Spirit, who gives the Sovereign Pontiff the help he needs so that the grace and truth of Christ may be poured forth fully and generously into the hearts of men.

(j) Given the multiplicity of the functions that relate to the Petrine office, the Sovereign Pontiff is given a *multiple charism*: the power of the Spirit accompanies him in *all* his functions, as teacher, priest and pastor. The charism of holiness is not, however, proper to the Pope, even though holiness is a most important contributory factor to the effectiveness of his ministry.

(k) In the Sovereign Pontiff more than in any other member, three essential characteristics of the Church must be realised: unity, apostolicity and catholicity. And this takes place through the work of the Spirit. One can say, therefore, that the papacy is the *charismatic instrument* for the preservation and development of unity, apostolicity and catholicity. These characteristics of the Church could be conceived of as purely sociological qualities, inherent in the Church as a social grouping, in which case the papacy, which has an important function to perform in contributing to their realisation, would likewise have only a sociological and historical justification. But if unity, apostolicity and catholicity are considered from the *theological* point of view, as supernatural properties which belong to the Church through the will and free gift of the Holy

Spirit, then even that most effective instrument for their preservation, which is the papacy, finds its justification in the will and assistance of the Holy Spirit. The papacy is in fact a gift that the Spirit makes to the Church in order to preserve the *unity* of faith, keep her faithful to the *apostolic heritage* and help her grow towards that *catholicity* which is proper to her as an instrument of salvation for all mankind.

3. *The assistance of the Holy Spirit*

(*l*) Tradition has always included *indefectibility* and *infallibility* among the essential marks of the Church. The best qualified bearer and guarantor of the mark of infallibility is the Pope, but it is part of the papal charism only in subordination to and as an explicit expression of that constantly attentive assistance which the Holy Spirit gives to his Bride, in order to preserve her from error and make her progress in truth and goodness. The infallibility of the Church assumes a sacramental and visible form in the episcopal college, which can act either as such, or else in the person of its head, the Sovereign Pontiff.

(*m*) The dynamics of the assistance given by the Holy Spirit to the Church and to her individual members is mysterious, as for that matter is the reality of the Spirit himself. The possibility is not to be ruled out, and indeed it is right to suppose, that in some cases the Spirit acts as exclusive agent, intervening in an absolutely extraordinary way: immediately and directly (in a vision or else by means of an *interior inspiration*) he makes his will known to the Sovereign Pontiff. This it seems is what happened when Pope John XXIII decided to convene the second Vatican Council. In such cases the initiative rests entirely with the Holy Spirit. Normally, however, the Spirit relies on the active contribution of the human factor, as is befitting for the Church, which is a communion of persons, of free, intelligent beings who are masters of themselves and fashioners of their own history, their own destiny.

(*n*) The human contribution cannot be reduced merely to listening to the Word the Spirit pronounces on the hearts of the faithful and humbly obeying his commands; it also involves a *laborious search* for the will of the Holy Spirit through intelligent reading of the signs of the times and the discerning use of all the resources that nature, science (particularly the human sciences) and technology placed at one's disposal. This principle applies to all the Church's institutions, but it does so above all to the papacy, on account of the profound importance of the papal ministry.

(*o*) In order to hear the voice of the Spirit and to give effect to the charism which is proper to him, it is not enough that the Pope should pray, mediate, do penance, celebrate Mass and recite the Divine Office, because as a rule not even he is granted the privilege of direct communication with the Holy Spirit: there is *no direct line* between heaven and the Vatican. In order to listen attentively to the Word of God and to work effectively for the coming of his Kingdom, the Pope must make use of all the resources available to him, both inside and outside the Church, by consulting with his brothers in the episcopate, with theologians, priests and lay people, with scientists and philosphers, with politicans and so on. More than any other member of the Church the Pope has the obligation to be a 'hearer of the word': he must have a strong sense of listening to the Holy Spirit. Even for the Pope the normal way in which the Spirit manifests himself is through faith and the charisms of the People of God, and in particular through the saints, who are those on whom the Spirit has poured forth extraordinary gifts and charisms. One thinks here of the humble way in which Pope Eugenius III listened to St Bernard or Gregory IX to St Catherine of Siena. They are models which all pontiffs should keep before themselves continually: the saints should be their preferred counsellors.

4. CONCLUSION

In concrete terms, at the level of experience, in what circumstances can one assume that the Pope is acting through the power of the Spirit? It would be impossible here to give a list of the cases in which the presence of the Spirit is clearly manifest. The most one can do is to indicate a few reasonably enlightening criteria.

We know that the Spirit is essentially *power of liberation from slavery* (in its many manifestations) and *force of renewal and resurrection.* Consequently, the Pope acts under the impulse of the Spirit when he makes active and efficacious the power of the 'new creation': when he intervenes courageously in favour of the liberation of the oppressed, the granting of equal treatment to those who are discriminated against, the integration of the marginalised, the education of the ignorant, the health of the sick, the reconciliation of enemies, the protection of the weak, peace among warring groups, and so on and so forth. The Pope acts in the power of the Spirit when, as a result of his watchful initiatives men do not resign themselves to the slavery of death, sin, ignorance, violence, lust and egoism, but hope instead in the triumph of life, truth and love; when, through his word and his example the forces of the Kingdom of God take their stand against the malign forces of sorrow, slavery and death. Today, as in the time of St Paul, the term 'malign forces' refers not only to idols and religious demons but also, as Harvey Cox has so lucidly demonstrated in *The Secular City,* to the divinised forces of modern civilisation—race, sex, pleasure, work, progress, technology, politics, sport which corrupt and paralyse human freedom.

I would like to conclude by recalling a recent example of an action which was carried out under the impulse of the Spirit and left the world greatly moved: the courageous appeal made by Pope John Paul II at the moment of his election to all men throughout the world, believers or non-believers, to open themselves once again, without any trace of fear, to the word of Christ. In these solemn circumstances the Pope said: 'Do not be afraid. Open wide the doors for Christ. To his saving power open up the boundaries of states, economic and political systems, the vast fields of culture, civilisations and development. Do not be afraid. Christ knows "what is in man". He alone knows it. So often today man does not know what is within him, in the depths of his mind and heart. So often he is uncertain about the meaning of his life on this earth. He is assailed by doubt, a doubt that turns into despair. We ask you, therefore, we beg with humility and trust, let Christ speak to man. He alone has the words of life, yes, of eternal life.'

When, as in this case, the Pope becomes the humble representative of the person of Christ and proclaims his Gospel so clearly, the power of the Spirit is certainly with him.

Translated by Sarah Fawcett

Hermann Häring

The Role of the Spirit
in the Legitimation of
Ecclesial Office

THIS ARTICLE is about the legitimisation of ecclesial office from the Roman Catholic point of view.[1] This office is therefore taken in the way Catholics understand it: a question of bishops and priests who, all in their own way, exercise authority over the local or regional churches either directly or by participation. The question of the relation between 'the Spirit and ecclesial office' as implied in the heading concentrates specifically on what is called the 'Roman question'. What does this imply? Have Catholic theologians paid more attention than others to the 'spiritual' aspect of the office and found a universally valid solution? Or have they rather used the Spirit for ideological purposes and so reduced him to an inspirational prop for a bureaucratic mentality? Both these questions only reflect prejudices and are therefore wrong. The Catholic Church only reflects a common ecumenical problem, sharpened in a particularly painful way because of past history. The ignoring of the Spirit played as great a part as unwarranted appealing to Him. This needs some clarification.

1. WHO NEEDS THIS LEGITIMISING BY THE SPIRIT?

1. *The Spirit and the Church of Jesus Christ*

All Christians unanimously confess that Christ is present to us and operative in us in the Spirit. This means that the whole of Christ's operative presence, whether in word, deed or the Church, must be seen as the fruit of the Spirit. He alone enables us to speak and act in the name of Christ. This implies that, historically speaking, the Spirit is the ultimate court of appeal, and that, in the field of interpretation, this Spirit embodies the last word where Christian legitimacy is concerned. Here one may refer to the 'apostolic council' (Acts 15:6-29), or the laying on of hands in Samaria (Acts 8:14-17), or the doctrine of the sacraments, or a universally Christian understanding of word and scripture. For Christians there is no legitimisation outside the Spirit (1 Cor. 2:14-16).

The question, therefore, of the 'spiritual' legitimacy of our institutions and achievements is by no means a specifically Catholic issue, but one that is supremely *ecumenical*.[2] Thus the relationship between the Spirit and ecclesial office is a question which has to be faced by all the churches requiring a theological basis for their offices and not satisfied with a purely pragmatic approach. This is because all of them start from the experiential fact that any presence of Christ, including his Church, necessarily implies his Spirit.

2. The Spirit and ecclesial office

In the early Church there were three basic elements. Apart from word and sacrament, there was the (episcopal) office, and so we had *confessio, communio and oboedientia*. But this office only means anything if it can be experienced in the Spirit, and therefore is accepted as having authority in the Spirit. People saw the bishop as the head and the 'prince' of the community, knew about a handing on of the Spirit, and even a kind of succession in the 'charis'. Eastern theology took over this conviction and stresses the point that the pneumatic aspect of ecclesial office should not be neglected.[3] The linking of the Spirit with the office is therefore a patristic and particularly *eastern legacy* and in no way special to the West. The claim that the office is linked with the Spirit is therefore rooted in a common tradition, still actually alive in the East. It grew out of the experience that the office belongs to the Church of Jesus Christ and must therefore be positively related to the Spirit.

3. The Spirit and the authoritative word

In the critical explanation of his position with regard to the traditional Church Luther understood the Church as the *creatura verbi*, the creature of the word. For him the Church is unalterably the *locus* where God's justifying word is constantly witnessed to afresh and seized in faith. The Church is therefore essentially an event and, in the language of St Augustine, invisible. And so the appeal to the Spirit is no longer merely a crucial stage in the legitimation of ecclesial offices but radically distances them all.[4] And yet, even the churches of the reformation have a particular office for leading the community, preaching the word and administering the sacraments. Even they cannot do without a visible organisation of the community. But how are they going to provide some spiritual legitimation for their ecclesial society and their ecclesial offices (apart from the universal priesthood)?

And so we are faced with the same question of the link between the Spirit and ecclesial office: it is not merely a pre-reformation problem but a genuine issue for the *churches of the reformation*. And it starts from the experience that Spirit and office will drift apart when the word of God is no longer relevant in office.

4. *Spiritual Legitimisation*

So today an ecumenically responsible theology must start from this polarisation between an ecclesial experience of the Spirit and a criticism of the churches based on this Spirit. Is it possible to avoid both a naïve identification of Spirit and office and opposing them in an irreconcilable contradiction? This is precisely what Catholic theology ought to attempt with its clear-cut theology of ecclesial office. It is therefore not astonishing that the matter of a well thought out spiritual legitimation of ecclesial office is most hotly debated today in the *Catholic Church*.[5] For today we are in principle still in agreement with the Eastern churches while at the same time we are vitally affected by the questions raised by the Reformation. The question of 'Spirit and office' is therefore an ecumenical problem which has to be effectively dealt with especially by *Catholic theology*. For the Spirit should at the same time legitimise the office and limit it. Yet, at first sight it would seem that Catholic theology is hardly ready for this legitimisation of the office by the Spirit.

2. THE FULLNESS OF POWER FLOWING FROM CHRIST

1. *The growth of legalisation* . . .

From the second century on the Church found great difficulty in coping with spiritual experience within the Church. Charismatics, prophets and an enthusiastic Christianity clearly created unrest and endangered the purity of the faith. And so it came to be seen as the bishops' task to see to it that these spiritual claims and movements were within the terms of the faith handed on by the Apostles. If you therefore appealed to the Spirit, you had to subject yourself to the judgement of the bishops who felt themselves bound by the canon of the truth as shown in Christ. The *spiritual legitimisation* of the office remained rightly orientated to the Christ-centred truth of the gospel since only the Spirit of Christ could be the true Spirit.[6] But what in the old Church was still carried out as a genuine spiritual task of the episcopal office assumed in the middle ages an increasingly juridical and canonical character. In the light of a powerful hierarchy, provided with all kinds of public power, the Church came to be seen as a legally organised society. Subjects which were originally part of Christian spiritual anthropology (e.g., Jer. 1:10; 2 Cor. 2:15; 6:3; 1 Pet. 2:9) were taken into the area of the law. 'Legalism is typical of an ecclesiology which is no longer related to spiritual anthropology and where the term "ecclesia" has come to mean less the body of the faithful than the system, the "apparatchik", the impersonal administration of the legal set-up!' And so spiritual authority became a *legalistic authority* 'which exists primarily and before everything else for its own sake'.[7]

Today the theology of ecclesial office suffers from a crisis of which the symptoms are too well known to need more than a brief mention. The general theory of ecclesial office shrivelled up and was reduced to the doctrine about the sacramental (ordained) priesthood.[8] The concepts of mission and succession were steam-rollered under the dominant idea of a legalism which saw the office only in a horizontal way and which became ever more papalistic until Pius XII. The *potestas ordinis,* which had a sacramental foundation, and the *potestas iurisdictionis,* which only had a canonical basis, drifted widely apart. The occasional addition of some fundamental *potestas magisterii* only served to make people more worried about where they had to look for the inner spiritual unity of the Church's authority.[9]

In so far as the nature of ecclesial office is concerned, the traditional textbooks of even this century have astonishingly little to say about the Holy Spirit and then *only incidentally,* something on the lines of John 20:22f. Traditional ecclesiologies only treat of the infallibility of the pope and the councils (a central proposition based on the Spirit) at the end and after a number of other subjects. In the same way Vatican I saw papal infallibility simply as a consequence of the pope's primacy in jurisdiction.

2. . . . *instead of spiritual legitimisation*

And so it is today universally admitted that this one-sided juridical understanding of ecclesial office shows a *lack of spiritual insight.* It is true that even this understanding of the office has always gone hand in hand with a serious religious attitude towards it in practice. One only has to think, for instance, of the pious attitude towards the Church of Ignatius of Loyola. But the Spirit was no longer pointed to as the ultimate criterion of the legitimisation of the office—on the contrary, he was forgotten. The central concept of apostolic succession at its various levels (being sent in Christ, having authority in the Spirit, and preserving the apostolic faith) became shallow through a poor application of christob gy in order to arrive at a confirmation of a juridical succession in office. The foreground was no longer occupied by the question of the inner legitimisation but rather by the question of a legality which was external, could be historically explained and was open to appeal. And so the office became, without people realising it, the institution which legitimised the Spirit instead of the other way round. And thus it appeared that the Spirit was superseded by the office.

From these conflicting trends of the Catholic Church and its theology Vatican II began to develop a saner teaching. Both before and after the (episcopal) office was based on the apostolic, sacramentally transmitted succession. And so, before and after, the supreme authority of the Christ, who sent his apostles, was shown to be the basis of the legitimisation of ecclesial office. It had therefore not been forgotten that the spirits have to be discerned in a specific Christian way, and that therefore only the Spirit of Christ can be the legitimising authority of the ecclesial office.[10] But it was also realised that the Spirit operates not only in the hierarchy but above all in the whole people of God; that the fruit of the Spirit does not mean domination but service and community, and that this Spirit operates also outside the Catholic Church, and first of all in other churches and ecclesial communities.[11] But this makes it obvious that it is the Spirit of Christ who at the same time legitimises and indicates the limits of the ecclesial office.

3. THE PROMISE OF THE SPIRIT

1. *The challenge of our age*

Nevertheless, the legalism of the office never managed to expunge all memory of the Spirit from the treatises on the Church. Never driven out, though reduced to alien status, the *spiritual dimension* of ordination and sacraments remained a value for the ordained office-holders as the mediators and administrators of these events. The laying on of hands by the bishop mediates the power of the Spirit, and makes bishops and priests men of the Spirit. The memory of the Pentecostal event which the Fathers, following Luke's presentation of it, saw as the birth of the Church, remained alive, even though the consequences were often ignored. Tradition saw the Church not only as the body of Christ but also as the bride of the Spirit. And it is worth remembering that Pius XII at the peak of papalism described the Spirit as the soul of the body of Christ.[12]

Yet, even these images and general ideas usually led to an uncritical hierarchisation of the Church. They could moreover lend all legalism a touch of *mysticism* and *depth* which made it well-nigh unquestionable. 'Whoever met the apostles, met the Holy Spirit Himself', said Schmaus more or less talking about their doctrinal authority in the Church.[13] There was therefore a danger that this kind of spiritual understanding of ecclesial office might even reinforce that identification of the Catholic Church with salvation *tout court.*

The *new situation* was therefore of decisive importance since it forced the Catholic Church to come to terms with modern thought and the awakening of historical awareness. *First of all,* the question was no longer the Church's claim to power, nor even the legitimacy of particular Christian churches, but the fact that *the Christian message claimed to be the truth.* Criticism of the Christian faith had to be met by establishing in general that, according to the structure of its offices, this Church was not only called but also enabled to preach the divine truth. The appeal to the Spirit (John 14:17; 16:13) now had become the key to a legitimisation which held the whole theory of the Church's office as in a clamp.[14]

Secondly, the debate is no longer about whether to say 'yes' or 'no' to truths that can be fixed like statistics, nor even about the choice between a Catholic or Protestant, but in any case fixed system of pronouncements, but about *the historicity of the truth itself.* How can one still meaningfully talk about a preservation of the true faith, when binding statements of the faith have only gradually become crystallised or have been modified? This subject which was already brought up in the sixteenth century, was energetically taken up by the theologians of Tübingen in the nineteenth century and till the middle of our own century created a lot of controversy when people discussed what was gathered under the heading of 'development of dogma'. But anyone who wants to tackle this issue from the angle of the Spirit will have to see this Spirit not merely as the guarantor but as the very *source of truth,* letting all new pronouncements freely flow from himself, whether as a logical or an organic development of the old truths. This Spirit must therefore be understood not merely as providing some kind of assistance but as the very principle of life in so far as the Church is concerned. He is not merely there to prevent error (as in the official teaching of infallibility) but constantly discloses the truth of Christ in a way which is positive and always new.

One can therefore see why precisely in the nineteenth century there was a re-discovery of the part played by the Spirit and why (as implied in the theology of Tübingen) this very fact demanded a new approach to the question about the nature of the Church.[15] This also makes it obvious why, in view of the definition of infallibility of 1870, the relation between Spirit and office became an outstanding topic in the controversy between Catholicism and Protestantism. Finally, all this should also make it clear that this controversy can no longer remain limited locally to some particular topic of ecclesiology. It should be treated as the basic issue of theology at large, and should concentrate on: (1) how the *Church* can be the locus of Christian truth, and (2) how this truth becomes operative through the ecclesial *office.*

2. *Church and office*

So we have here a dual question which for a long time had not been properly diagnosed in Catholic theology nor adequately co-ordinated in the Protestant argument. To illustrate this one might start from the basic ecumenical conviction that the Spirit has been *given to the Church* through word and sacrament.

It has been a long-standing tendency in *Catholic theology* to apply this basic conviction from the universal Church to its offices by analogical reasoning. Up till today it has therefore been inclined to deny this basic conviction to all those who did not want to apply it to ecclesial office (by way of a kind of representative duplication). One could illustrate this thesis by referring to the problems of the canon of the scriptures, the Church's tradition and the ever actual obligatory doctrine of the faith, as well as to the question of the apostolic succession of the bishops.

But what in this theology looked like ecclesiological consistency and courageous obedience was hardly borne out by the manifold consequences which the presence of the Spirit as such should have throughout the Church, nor was it worked out in its official teaching. This way of thinking was significantly revealed in another context by the statement of Vatican I that the pope enjoys 'that (!) infallibility' with which Christ 'wanted to see his church equipped'. It is precisely 'that' infallibility which was nowhere mentioned—and this is a weakness which besets the whole definition. Protestant theology has always had great difficulty in trying to legitimise the above-mentioned spiritual-ecclesial realities (tradition, office, apostolic succession and the canonicity of Scripture) on the basis of the Spirit in a way which was specific and historically adequate. With the same wretched consistency and use of analogy it was thought that they had to deny the (visible) Church as a whole what they would not credit the ecclesial office with in this way. And so the idea of a (visible) universal Church became suspect as an official structure which had forgotten all about the Spirit. Thus 'in Protestantism the whole problem of the Church's teaching . . . became in this respect the very expression of the Church's teaching'.[16] This situation, however, was reflected in the corresponding fact that anyone who still managed to see some spiritual sense in the visible structures of their church (the offices and the claim to the formulation of the truth) could become suspected of a kind of bad and triumphalistic paracatholicism. The most prominent victim (and an indication of the weakness of this position) was Luke, the theologian of the Church's Spirit or, if preferred, of a Spirit-orientated and yet distinctly christological ecclesiology.[17]

Yet, it was in Luke, the 'early Catholic', that one could learn about a specific and basic spiritual experience which could be put into practice and of which one could analyse the consequences: the Church of Jesus

Christ, the fraternal community of the faithful, is born of his Spirit and therefore the qualified locus of his activity. The office-holders, however, labour in the strength of the Spirit inasmuch as they are 'eye-witnesses' of Jesus Christ during his life and proclaim his message, and therefore are entitled to be listened to in the community and to be taken seriously. All communities find their unity (also in the spatial sense) in a place, the place of their (spiritual) origin. The promise of the Spirit therefore also holds good for those who hold an ecclesial office. He it is who enables them to fulfil their function in a spiritual manner. In accordance with later practice the Spirit is therefore transmitted to them symbolically through the laying on of hands.[18]

4. HOW IS THE COMMUNITY GUIDED IN THE POWER OF THE SPIRIT?

If therefore the Spirit legitimises the ecclesial office, how does it work? In some eight propositions I will try to give a Catholic, ecumenically responsible answer to this question.

1. *The Catholic heritage*

First of all, apart from the peculiar case of the definition of infallibility (with its theory of a merely negative assistance of the Spirit) Catholic tradition has nowhere concentrated on, or defined the relationship between Spirit and office in a way which was binding on all. But Catholic tradition always assumed that the Spirit was *promised to those who held office,* and therefore assists them in fulfilling their task. From this the office-holder derives a genuine spiritual authority.

Secondly, history shows that the spiritual dimension of the ecclesial office can be curtailed or forgotten and that at the same time the appeal to the Spirit can be abused by the office for its own self-justification. It is therefore imperative that in future the *spiritual character* of the office be *recognised without any limitation,* and at the same time be made dependent on that *listening to the Spirit* which we are qualified to do through the promise of the Spirit.

Thirdly, the same history of the ecclesial office shows that its christological legitimisation has often become a legal argument and that, as a result, the constant one-sided referring to a historical legality threatened to stifle the question about the inner legitimacy. The notion of apostolic succession must therefore be understood as *continuity in the Spirit of Jesus Christ* and the only way of legitimising it is through *obedience to the Christian message.*

2. *In the community and over the community*

Fourthly, the Spirit of Jesus Christ is given to all those who are baptised in view of each one's own calling as the radical 'subjective reality of revelation' (K. Barth). This also holds for those in office. Therefore, in so far as those in office are bound to fulfil functions which concern the community as a whole (the service of word and sacrament, representation and guidance of the community, care for the universal Church) they hold a position of direct spiritual *authority over the whole community.* This is a justifiable basic experience which has been continuous in the Catholic Church and is constantly re-asserted in the ordination of priests and bishops.

Fifth proposition. This spiritual authority of the office-holder is, however, counterbalanced by the equally direct authority given to all the baptised where their own calling is concerned. So, while there is a qualitative difference in the function (with regard to the whole community), in principle the spiritual legitimisation is nevertheless the same. From this angle then the leadership office given to the Church is simply *one charism among others,* a charism which gives them their place in the community.

Sixth proposition. All have been given the Spirit in so far as they constitute the community of the faithful. For them, including the office-holders, the ultimate common and unifying and therefore valid criterion is their *service to the community,* their faith and their love. Whether the function can show itself as *having* this inner legitimacy of a spiritual service depends on whether it manages to do what it is supposed to do, and to find this out will take time.

3. *How does one serve the Spirit of Jesus Christ?*

Seventh proposition. The existence and function of particular offices which have been—and are still being—moulded in the course of the centuries (think of the Petrine office, the episcopacy and the priesthood) cannot simply be deduced from the logical premises of the Christian message. They have to be seen as part and parcel of the way in which the Spirit operates in history and have to be taken seriously according to any new understanding of the gospel. In so far as Catholic experience is concerned there has been an uninterrupted conviction that the Church's structure, based on the Petrine episcopal principle, regardless of any queries about the origin of this principle and possible exceptions, should be maintained b r the sake of the Christian faith and an ecumenically unified church, and thus serving the concern about the true Spirit.

Eighth proposition. In view of the spiritual situation and the world-wide problems of our time the churches and their officers will have to be really concerned about the possibility that the Spirit may get dissolved into a kind of false unity, and see to it that there will be a new awakening of charisms, protected and strengthened for the messianic message of Christian hope.

The spiritual authority of the office-holder will prove itself by its *ability to kindle the power of the Spirit* and to win people for Jesus Christ.

How then does the Spirit legitimise the ecclesial office? He does it by not denying his help to those whom the Church calls to a particular function in the name of Christ, and by reminding them of this same Jesus Christ in a way that is constantly new. Faith in the Spirit is expressed as trust in the power of the word. This leads to the trust that the Church of Jesus Christ cannot perish. The question therefore cannot be a matter of declaring that particular Church authorities can legitimise the Spirit or of putting the Spirit at the disposal of such authorities. On the contrary, *any doubt* about whether the Spirit really operates in such ecclesiastically integrated offices can only be overcome by trusting the power of the Spirit in these offices. When it has become clear that this confidence does not lie in overruling the Spirit but is subject to the authority of the Spirit we may still see the growth of an understanding which is ecumenically important.

Translated by Theo Westow

Notes

1. The problem of the Petrine office has been left out here as it is dealt with in the preceding article. In my article 'Kann ein Petrusdienst in der Kirche einen Sinn haben? Versuch einer katholischen Antwort', in *Concilium* 7 (1971), the Petrine office was said to be 'inalienable'. The sentence should read: 'The Petrine office in not *unalterable* and can take on many forms.'

2. V. Vajta 'Der Heilige Geist und die Strukturen der Kirche', in H. Meyer a.o. *Wiederentdeckung des Heiligen Geistes. Ökumenische Perspektiven* 6 (Frankfurt 1974) pp. 77-96.

3. For the history of the ecclesial office, see Congar (note 7); J. Ratzinger *Das neue Volk Gottes. Entwürfe zur Ekklesiologie* (Düsseldorf 1964) pp. 73-245; J. Madey 'Das Charisma des Apostolischen Amtes im Denken und Beten der Ostkirchen', in *Catholica* 27 (1973) pp. 263-279; E. P. Siman 'L'expérience de l'Esprit par l'Eglise d'après la tradition syrienne d'Antioche' in *Théologie Historique* 15 (Paris 1971).

4. A survey of the present very complicated debate can be found in H. Schütte

Amt, Ordination und Sukzession im Verständnis evangelischer und katholischer Exegeten und Dogmatiker der Gegenwart sowie in Dokumenten ökumenischer Gespräche (Düsseldorf 1974) pp. 17-211.

5. H. Küng *Die Kirche. Ökumenische Forschungen* I, 1 (Freiburg 1967) pp. 181-244; see Y. Congar's remarks in *Rev. des Sc. Philos. et Théol.* 53 (1959) pp. 693-706.

6. H. v. Campenhausen *Kirchliches Amt und geistliche Volmacht in den ersten drei Jahrhunderten* (Beiträge zur hist. Theol. 14, Tübingen 1963); J. Martin *Die Genese des Amtspriestertums in der frühen Kirche* (Quaest. Disp. 48, Freiburg 1972).

7. There is an excellent survey by Y. Congar 'The historical development of authority in the Church. Points for reflection' in *Problems of Authority* (ed. by J. M. Todd, London and Baltimore 1962) pp. 119-156, esp. pp. 140 and 141.

8. K. J. Becker *Wesen und Vollmachten des Priestertums nach dem Lehramt* (Qu. Disp. 47, Freiburg 1970).

9. See, e.g., J. B. Franzelin's op. posth. *Theses de Ecclesia Christi* (Rome 1887) pp. 43-64. For the not yet fully understood concept of the 'magisterium', see Y. Congar 'The history of the word "magisterium"', in *Concilium* 12 (1976).

10. C. Heitmann and H. Mühlen (ed.) *Erfahrung und Theologie des Heiligen Geistes* (Hamburg/Münich 1974), esp. pt. II, pp. 81-147.

11. Chapters 2, 4 and 5 of the Constitution on the church, *Lumen Gentium,* and ch. 1 of the Decree on Ecumenism, *Unitatis Redintegratio,* are important.

12. A good survey can be found in M. Schmaus *Katholische Dogmatik* III/1 (5th ed. Munich 1958) par. 169b and 170, pp. 239-391. Also important is H. U. v. Balthasar *Pneuma und Institution. Skizzen zur Theologie IV* (Einsiedeln 1974).

13. Op. cit. p. 358.

14. For the shift in the debate in recent times, see P. Eicher *Offenbarung. Prinzip neuzeitlicher Theologie* (Munich 1977) pp. 71-162; K. Barth *Die Kirchliche Dogmatik* I/2 (5th ed. Zurich 1960) par. 20 'Die Autorität in der Kirche' pp. 598-740.

15. One may illustrate this by referring to J. A. Möhler *Die Einheit in der Kirche oder das Prinzip des Katholizismus, dargestellt im Geiste der Kirchenväter der ersten drei Jahrhunderte* (Tübingen 1825; Cologne 1957); H. Schell *Das Wirken des dreieinigen Gottes* (Mainz 1885) esp. pp. 512-622; J. R. Geiselmann *Die katholische Tübinger Schule. Ihre theologische Eigenart* (Freiburg 1964); for Möhler see also Schmaus op. cit. pp. 341-345.

16. G. Ebeling *Wort Gottes und Tradition. Studien zu einer Hermeneutik der Konfessionen* (2nd ed. Göttingen 1966) p. 167.

17. E. Käsemann *Die Johannesjünger in Ephesus: Exegetische Versuche und Besinnungen* I (2nd ed. Göttingen 1966) pp. 158-168; id. *Der Ruf der Freiheit* (5th ed. Tübingen 1972) ch. 5: 'Verkirchlichte Freiheit' pp. 165-189. For the problem at large, see H. J. Schmitz *Frühkatholizismus bei Adolf v. Harnack, Rudolf Sohm und Ernst Käsemann* (Düsseldorf 1977) pp. 145-201.

18. H. Conzelmann *Die Mitte der Zeit. Studien zur Theologie des Lukas* (5th ed. Tübingen 1964).

Harding Meyer

A Protestant Attitude

1. A STRANGE QUESTION?

Without wishing to abandon the theme of the discussion—indeed, it is part of a Protestant attitude towards it—one is forced to say at the outset that the immediate concentration of the overall theme 'Office and Spirit' in the concept of 'The Spirit as Legitimation of Office' sounds strange, even dubious, to Protestant ears. That the Spirit has something to do with 'office'—and here we can agree with H. Häring—will certainly not be disputed, even by those who hold to a consistently functional under-standing of office, which is completely determined by the concept of the priesthood of all believers. The basic question of the legitimation of office, at least in the sense of the ever open question concerning the correct exercise of office, is thus all the more aptly posed for Protestant thinking.

But that the Spirit is the *authority* which 'legitimises' office is a concept—and here we must reject Häring's view—which cannot readily be ratified and adopted on the Protestant side. The idea that the Spirit 'legitimises' office seems to Protestant and reformed thinking to point rather in three highly dubious directions: in the direction of a 'donatist' understanding of office, in which the personal sanctity of the office bearer represents a decisive legitimation; of an 'enthusiastic' or 'pentecostal' view of the office bearer as the inspired charismatic *par excellence*; or of the 'Roman' view of office. 'The Spirit as the legitimation of office' appears to Protestant thinking not as a 'proper' question or as 'our own' problem, but rather as someone else's problem.

A Protestant attitude therefore cannot ignore the fact that this is, primarily, someone else's problem; in this context, Rome's. However, that attitude would be short-sighted if it did not see in this 'alien' question also a question directed at itself. What follows will, as far as possible, concern itself with both these aspects.

2. THE OBLIGATION AND FREEDOM OF THE SPIRIT—
THE PROTESTANT/REFORMED VIEW

1. *The opus proprium of the Spirit*

According to reformed thinking, the *opus proprium* of the Spirit is that process which leads from the 'act' of salvation accomplished in Jesus Christ to the (believing) 'acceptance' of that act. This is not primarily a question of bridging a 'historical gap' between then and now, but in overcoming an 'existential gap'; in the development of the 'factum' to the 'usus facti'; from 'salvation accomplished' by Christ to 'sanctification'; from 'treasure obtained' to 'treasure employed', as Luther says in the Large Catechism. In this sense the Holy Spirit is the 'sanctifying' Spirit, just as God the Father is 'creator' and God the Son, 'redeemer'.[1]

2. *Christological reference*

This work of the Spirit, however, is not unmediated. It takes place in the dialectic of obligation and freedom, a dialectic which may develop, in the first place, on the basis of a primary and essential obligation of the Spirit, namely, the connection with or reference to the once-for-all act of reconciliation by God in Christ. There can be no doubt about this fundamental 'christological',[2] even 'christocentric'[3] orientation of the Protestant/reformed view of the Spirit. So when, in the context of the dispute over the 'Filioque', this christological reference of the Spirit is called in question, the insistence of the reformed side on the 'Filioque' must, presumably, be emphasised. The Spirit is the Spirit of Christ; he brings us to Christ, and without him we do not come to Christ. 'I believe that it is not through my own reason or strength that I believe in or can come to Jesus Christ, my Lord, but that the Holy Spirit has called me through the gospel . . .'[4]—thus Luther's Small Catechism describes the work of the Spirit. The Heidelberg Catechism (question 53) says the Spirit 'gives me, by true faith, a share in Christ and all his benefits'. How far this christological connection with or reference to the Spirit leads to a weakening of the doctrine of the Trinity and a limiting of pneumatology has not yet been decided, but it remains an open question, which it is not possible to discuss here.

On the basis of this essential connection or reference point of the Spirit the question arises, how does the Spirit perform his work; this, in other words, is the dialectic of freedom and obligation, of identification and difference.

3. *Church and Office as Instruments of the Spirit*

The Spirit does his 'work' in man, or—another way of saying it—man receives the Spirit through external, public, verifiable means; thus the reformers insist. But these means remain what they are, namely, 'means', 'instrumenta', over which the Spirit disposes, but which on their part cannot dispose over the Spirit. One may certainly say that the Spirit works through external, public, verifiable means, but one cannot say that the presence and use of those means signifies in each case the presence and effects of the Spirit. The sovereign freedom of the Spirit thus manifests itself not in the immediacy of his work but in its consistently mediated character, which is subject to the Spirit's freedom.

What are these 'means' of the Spirit? Briefly, to avoid long digressions and unnecessary repetition of what is said elsewhere in this journal: the Holy Spirit works through the *Church and its office*. Should that sound strange to Protestant, and perhaps even to Catholic, ears,[5] they will simply have to accustom themselves to it. The reformers not only did not dispute that the Spirit works through the Church and its office; they even emphatically asserted it along with the ancient Church and, when necessary, defended it. Taking up the words of the Apostles' Creed Luther says, in his Large Catechism, that the Spirit 'directs . . . sanctification by the following means; the communion of saints or the Christian Church, the forgiveness of sins, the resurrection of the body and eternal life; that is, he first leads us into his holy community and places us in the bosom of the Church, where he preaches to us and brings us to Christ'.[6] Article 5 of the Confession of Augsburg says the same of the Church's office: 'So that we may come to this (i.e., justifying) faith, God has instituted the office of preaching and has given the gospel and the sacraments. Through these means (*instrumenta*) God gives the Holy Spirit, who creates faith, where and when he will, in those who hear the gospel.'

4. *Critique of Rome: pneumatological maximalism*

The conviction that both the Church and its office are instruments of the Spirit did not prevent the reformers from drawing a critical distinction between themselves and the Roman Church and theology of their time with regard to the question of the relationship between Church and Spirit or office and Spirit. This was not because they understood the Church as a 'pneumatic phenomenon' and, in the name of the Spirit, rejected all ecclesial and official structures, institutions and law, thus understanding the Spirit as the 'legitimation of a critique of office'.[7] What they criticised in the Catholic definition of the relationship of the Church to both office and Spirit was not an undervaluing of the Spirit but rather something which could be described as 'pneumatological maximalism'. In this respect—as far as the reformers were concerned—'papists' and 'enthusiasts' were in agreement, and Luther, along with the written Lutheran confessions, was able to see 'in the papacy ... vain enthusiasm'.[8]

Y. Congar has shown, in the context of the Catholic/Protestant debate concerning scripture, tradition and the Church—which is of direct relevance to our theme—how the Reformation came about within a theological horizon which was essentially determined—and which remained determined both during and after the Council of Trent—by an 'ecclesiological pneumatology'.[9] One can interchange the noun and the adjective and say 'pneumatological ecclesiology', though orthodox theologians would probably dispute that. For it is important for Congar to demonstrate that the decisive motivation for attributing binding force for faith to the so-called 'oral traditions of the apostles', that is, the historical decrees and developments of the Church, is of a pneumatological nature: the Spirit dwells in the Church; he is—as the whole of medieval theology and not just the nineteenth century and Pius XII asserted—linked to it like the 'soul' to the 'body'; he directs it in its history and its decisions. For this reason these historical developments of the Church and its office must be accepted as every bit as binding on faith, 'with equal pious acceptance and reverence' (pari pictatis affectu et reverentia), as what holy scripture says, for both scripture and tradition originate ultimately in the same Spirit.[10]

This direct pneumatological legitimation of ecclesiastical decisions was disputed by the reformers.[11] It is not the place here to go into how personal religious experiences, pastoral responsibility, historical verification and theological reflection worked together; the fact remains that that old pneumatological concept of the Church—perhaps one should say that fundamental and uncritical trust in the Church, which was filled with and directed by the Spirit—collapsed with the reformers. They rejected the pneumatological argument which was set against their own criticism of the binding nature of ecclesiastical decisions. For example, Luther says, with reference to the Church's teaching of seven sacraments: 'The Church does not have the authority to give new divine promises of grace, as some claim, saying that whatever the Church has instituted is of no less authority than what is instituted by God, since the Church is governed by the Holy Spirit'.[12] Even Calvin does not allow the conviction that 'the Church is directed by the Spirit of God' to stand as a satisfactory argument for the truth and binding force of the Church's decrees.[13]

5. *The Spirit's subjection to the Word as 'legitimation'*

The Spirit alone is thus insufficient legitimation for the actions and decisions of the Church and its office, for even within the Church the necessity for discerning the spirits does not stop, and every claim to possession of the Spirit has to be tested. Thus the basic criterion is that of the christological reference of the Spirit and his work: 'He will bring to your remembrance all that I have said to you' (John 14:26). This 'christological criterion' is then immediately established as the criterion of the Spirit's 'subjection to the Word'.[14]

That the Spirit is at work in the Church and its office only when this reference to the Word is given and verifiable, was the argument of the reformers against both 'enthusiasts' and 'papists'. The basic motivation is thus completely identical with the concern of the Reformation itself; man's salvation proceeds only from the act of God in Christ, and this divine saving act is and remains God's prerogative, removed from the control of man, 'over against' him, 'extra nos'. Of course God, by the Spirit, makes use of human agents (Church, office, preaching, sacraments etc.), but these agents must retain the character of pure agents, so that the divine prerogative is not diminished by human act, nor salvation and the assurance of it put in question. Thus this work of the Spirit, which is accomplished by 'agents', is open to critical examination, and the criterion for this examination is its reference to Christ, which means, in fact, 'subjection to the Word'.

This subjection to the Word and reference to Christ, which comes to expression in it, of the work of the Spirit in and through Church and office were, in the opinion of the reformers, insufficiently regarded—even disregarded—by the Roman Church. All decisions of both Church and office which do not exhibit this reference to the Word cannot therefore be regarded as being legitimised by the Spirit. To this extent 'papacy' and 'enthusiasm' are similar; both lay claim to the Spirit, but since the element of reference to the Word is lacking, or is simply disregarded, the spirit is not the Spirit of the Lord, but a human spirit, 'man's own reason'.[15]

6. *Conclusion: Office of the Spirit—Office of the Word*

P. E. Persson reached the conclusion, in a controversial theological study some years ago, that 'office' in the Catholic Church was understood as 'office of the Spirit' and not as 'office of the Word', *and for this reason* it was not 'office of the Spirit'.[16]

One could say that here the quintessence of the traditional Protestant/reformed attitude towards the Catholic understanding of 'office and Spirit' comes to expression, in a heightened yet representative form. At the same time the proper Protestant/reformed view is also expressed, and thereby it becomes clear why the question concerning the 'Spirit as legitimation of office' seems at first so distant and strange to Protestant thinking. 'The Word legitimises the office as office of the Spirit'; that, in brief, is the conviction which has always been and which naturally remains so impressed upon reformed thinking, that all other approaches to this area of thought have first to remove that feeling of strangeness of which we spoke at the beginning.

3. QUESTIONS—REFLECTIONS—COMMON AREAS

The question arises, whether a Protestant attitude can still remain today at this position. Do not new developments in thought, in piety and in contacts between our churches make necessary a revision of this judgment? Perhaps even a critical reappraisal of their own understanding of 'Spirit and office' is required of Protestants.

1. *Spirit: reality or cipher?*

R. Prenter showed, in his study of Luther's witness to the Holy Spirit, that the idea of the Spirit is constitutive for the reformer's whole theology; that his view of the Spirit is both trinitarian and eschatological—in the salvation history sense; that he holds fast to the 'undiminished divinity' of the Spirit and, together with the Spirit's 'sovereignty', emphasises his 'reality' in such a way as can really only be compared with the 'days of primitive Christianity' and its 'powerful pneumatic realism'. All the significant points in Luther's understanding of the Spirit can really only be comprehended, according to Prenter, under the biblical and primitive Christian designation 'spiritus creator': 'the Holy Spirit is the tri-une God, actually present to us as "spiritus creator" in our death and in our lostness'.[17]

Prenter set this result of his studies against the view, represented, for example, by R. Otto, that the Spirit had no constitutive role in Luther's understanding of faith; it was simply an auxiliary construction, ultimately superfluous, since the function of the Spirit had been taken over by faith itself and by the Word.[18]

However convincing Prenter's work is as a study of Luther, it leaves untouched the urgent question, whether or not Christian communities and theologians in the reformed tradition have, in fact, stood in precisely the same position in which Rudolf Otto—erroneously—saw Luther as standing. Is the Spirit, in Protestant thinking generally, anything more than an additional cipher, dispensable if necessary, for the graciousness of salvation, the 'givenness' of faith and, above all, the self-authentication of the Word? This question must always be borne in mind by Protestants, for it is addressed to them as they examine how far their former critical attitude to the Catholic view is still tenable today.

2. *On the present Catholic view*

In attempting to examine the traditional Protestant attitude in the light of its present validity, the most natural approach is on the basis of the foregoing Catholic contributions.

(a) Confirmation of Protestant criticism . . .?

It is striking that both authors begin by distancing themselves quite emphatically from an earlier Catholic vew of office. Their reservations concern a primarily juridical understanding and contrast it with a more strongly pneumatically oriented view. That is quite plain in the case of B. Mondin, but even in H. Häring it is fairly prominent. That is to say, Catholic self-criticism seems at first to ignore the criticism of the reformers.

However, while Häring highlights straightaway the danger points of a naïve pneumatological legitimation of office (as a mystical deepening of the legalistic understanding), and therefore repeatedly emphasises that the Spirit does not only legitimise but also 'limits' office, there is much less of this critical reservation to be felt in the case of Mondin. Certainly he also emphasises, as does Häring, that the Spirit is given, in the first instance, to the whole people. The relation of Spirit to 'office' or 'papal office' is—'normally'!—not that of a direct line (Mondin). Assistance and legitimation of office by the Spirit occurs not separately from but in relation to the work of the Spirit within the whole people of God, and thus they 'limit' office (Häring). But only Häring really takes up the basic concern of the Reformation by the necessary alignment of the Spirit with the 'truth of the gospel'. Mondin, on the other hand, and to put it bluntly, flies right in the face of the reformers' criticism, precisely because his pneumatological understanding of the papacy bears traces of 'maximalism'. How can one say of the pope that he is given to the Church by the Holy Spirit in order to 'keep it true to its apostolic inheritance'? How can one say that it is the pope's duty to be a 'hearer of the Word' if one then points him to every possible thing through which the Spirit may speak—from his episcopal brethren and the saints, through the signs of the times, to the natural and human sciences, the philosophers and politicians—*except* the canon of apostolic scriptures? Is that the way in which the Spirit legitimises the pope as 'the clear proclaimer of the gospel'?

It is to be hoped that those on the Catholic side will understand that such a view does not seem particularly inviting for Protestant/reformed thinking to admit the 'Spirit as legitimation of office' or of 'the office of pope'. It is also to be hoped that the Catholic side will understand that, in the face of such statements, one can only repeat Luther's reproach: such a view of the papacy is 'vain enthusiasm'.

(b) . . . or a question addressed to Protestantism?

But how representative is this view? And, to be fair, how much does Mondin's argument leave unsaid about the specific point of our theme? In view of these questions, Häring's discussion appears all the more significant, for here the reformers' questions have been properly discussed, and yet, at the same time, answered in such a way as to allow the Protestant to see and understand himself not only as the one who asks the questions but also the one under questioning. The question which Häring poses for the Protestant understanding of Spirit and Church/office, and which is also being raised in other quarters, even among Protestants, is, how far has the concept of the Spirit's subjection to the Word increasingly denied to ecclesial realities (Church tradition, Church offices etc.) their pneumatic dimension? These were all conceded at the Reformation, even if it was thought that they were to be verified and 'legitimised' by the 'Word'. Another way of asking the same question would be, how can the 'subjection of the Word to the Spirit'[19] be conceived and taken as seriously as, at the same time, the subjection of the Spirit to the Word?

The challenge expressed in this question will certainly have to include other, more wide-reaching aspects than simply that of 'Spirit-Church-office'.[20] But it certainly does include this aspect and with it the appeal and the invitation to recognise again that the 'Word', through which the Spirit carries out his *opus proprium,* is itself bound to the Church as the locus and instrument of the Spirit. It is thus bound also to the people of God, to ecclesiastical offices and structures, to the Church's historical experiences, its decisions and creeds, as pneumatically determined realities. This can really only be denied if one instists upon a biblicist and exclusive equation of 'Word of God', 'holy scripture' and 'Spirit'—which is not the reformed view—or if one postulates a strangely unmediated and unhistorical relationship between the exegete and the text of holy scripture. This simply does not exist, for the simple reason that it cannot, however much it might be desired for purely polemical reasons.

However, if, with Luther, one understands the 'Word of God', which the Spirit uses in his *opus proprium,* as the 'living Word' of the gospel,[21] it immediately becomes clear that that Word is not isolated from those ecclesial realities to which, among others, office belongs.

3. *The overall framework: the problem of tradition*

All this leads our discussions to that total context in which they essentially belong, that is, in the comprehensive question, disputed by our two churches for centuries, of 'tradition', or the handing on of the gospel of Christ, which is the *opus proprium* of the Spirit.

During this long-standing debate, basic understandings have resulted which are of direct relevance for our theme. Here is not the place to draw up a list of these theological developments,[22] but, in conclusion, this much must be said: both Catholic and Protestant churches have rediscovered a theological understanding of the process of tradition which is common to both, in its broad outlines. It is determined by the following three elements: (1) the handing on of the gospel is always a human activity, but ultimately and in reality it is a work of the Holy Spirit; (2) it is a unified process in which not one single element (whether scripture or the teaching office) dominates the others, but, in their various proportions, all work together: the canon of holy scripture, the heritage of the historical experience and decrees of the Church and the living proclamation, confession, teaching and actions of the contemporary Church and its offices; (3) this process of tradition which is included in the pneumatological total aspect and determined by different but related elements exhibits in itself an 'order of precedence'. It is determined by the normative primacy of the apostolic scriptures, in which the connection of the present Church to its abiding origin both comes to expression and is guaranteed.

It is in the total context of this pneumatological, unified and internally structured understanding of tradition that the question of 'Spirit' and 'office' finds its proper place and its correct answer. It is quite understandable[23] that different emphases are possible and also that the relationship between Spirit and office may exhibit different nuances within the framework of such a common understanding of tradition. These differences are tolerable, as long as they do not lead again to breakdowns in communication and the consequent collapse of the pneumatological wholeness of the process of tradition and its proper internal order.

Translated by Martin Kitchen

Notes

1. *The Large Catechism,* Article 3, 35-37: *The Confessional Documents of the Evangelical Lutheran Church* ("CD"), (Göttingen 1953) p. 653f.

2. E. Kinder *The Doctrine of the Holy Spirit in the Lutheran Confessional Documents*: Fulda Books 15 (Berlin 1964) p. 9ff. G. Sauter *The Church in the Crisis of the Spirit: Church, Locus of the Spirit,* ed. W. Kasper and G. Sauter (Freiburg 1976) p. 80f.

3. R. Prenter *Spiritus Creator—Studies in Luther's Theology* (Munich 1954) p. 66 (see p. 42-67).

4. Explanation of Article 3, CD, p. 511f.

5. Certain of H. Häring's statements about the reformed view do create this suspicion.

6. Op. cit. p. 37—CD p. 654.

7. Häring's statement of reformed criticism tends too far in this direction.

8. CD p. 454f.

9. *La Tradition et les Traditions—Essai Historique* (Paris 1960) p. 222.

10. See Congar op. cit. pp. 213, 220, 227.

11. Even Congar clearly refers to the danger points of that old, fundamental concept, which he accepts. He speaks of the danger of 'levelling' (*aplatissement*) of the constitutive apostolic elements, op. cit. p. 222.

12. *The Babylonisch Captivity of the Church,* Weimarer Ausgabe 6, p. 560.

13. *Institutes of the Christian Religion* IV/8, p. 13.

14. See as in note 13.

15. Ibid.

16. *The Office of the Spirit—A Theological Sketch: Kerygma and Dogma* (1959) p. 99ff, esp. p. 116. Cf. E. Kinder op. cit. p. 27f.

17. Op. cit. p. 199, 202.

18. *Luther's Perception of the Holy Spirit* (Göttingen, 1898) esp. pp. 38ff and 49ff.

19. G. Sauter op. cit. p. 90.

20. See, for example, G. Sauter op. cit. pp. 91ff.

21. R. Prenter op. cit. pp. 107-132.

22. See H. Meyer *Ecumenical Reflection on the Problem of Tradition—A Balance Sheet: Gospel as History—Permanence and Change in the Handing on of the Gospel,* ed. V. Vajta (Göttingen 1974) pp. 187-219.

23. Ibid. p. 211ff.

Part IV

Spirit and Spirits:
The Question of the Charismatic Movement

Kilian McDonnell

The Experience of the
Holy Spirit in the
Catholic Charismatic Renewal

THOUGH A critical evaluation of the claims of those in the charismatic renewal regarding the experience of the Spirit is very much in place, my focus is the actual historical shape of that experience, its modalities and accents. My task is descriptive rather than critical.

Among New Testament exegetes it is a commonplace that 'long before the Spirit was a theme of doctrine he was a fact in the experience of the community' (Schweizer), or that 'the Church would have had no doctrine of the Spirit if it had not in the first place received an experience of the Spirit' (Barrett), or that the 'root of Paul's pneuma teaching lies in the experience of the Apostle' (Gunkel). This experience of the Spirit was not a peripheral adjunct but in some way defined what the community was: 'Experience of the Spirit is not merely one aspect of the new life of the believing community; it is the principle of it. It is that in which the new life consists' (Lampe).

Others have noted that at the conversion of the Galatians (therefore at the beginning of the Christian life) there must have been special works of the Spirit of a charismatic nature which demonstrated in a most concrete way that the truth of the gospel came from faith, not from the works of the law. What is certain is that works of the Spirit were 'visible, unusual, and impressive' (Kuss), not therefore something which would happen unnoticed. The reception of the Spirit and his gifts were verifiable. To state this is not to legislate an unvariable law, but to make an accurate historical observation. The charismatic renewal is suggesting that what was true at least for Paul (and Luke) has something to say to us today.

1. BAPTISM IN THE SPIRIT

The central charismatic experience is the baptism in the Holy Spirit,[1] which is usually seen as a breaking through to conscious awareness of the Spirit already received and present through Christian initiation, and is not a second baptism.

1. *An example . . .*

Here I give an actual account of the baptism in the Spirit of an educated Catholic layman, father of a family, and a successful businessman, an account which would not be atypical. He had been active in his parish and frequented the sacraments, but he felt spiritually unfulfilled. In his own words:

'I was really hungry for God. Though I had long wanted the baptism in the Holy Spirit I had a difficult time giving up things in my life which were displeasing to the Lord. Once when I was traveling in my car on a business trip I began to turn to the Lord and implore him as I drove along to baptise me in the Holy Spirit. And I told the Lord that he could have anything in my life that he wanted. I would hold on to nothing. Then, right there in the car, the presence of Jesus fell on me. It really enveloped me entirely; my spirit, but also my body. I pulled over to the side of the road and parked as wave on wave of his love washed over me from within. All I could think about were two things: "He loves me." "His love really is without end." This conviction was so deep, his presence so immediate, the touch from within so powerful that at that moment I felt as though I could never turn again from him in sin. I began to pour out my praise and adoration in tongues and very quietly, but without shame, to weep tears of joy. After some forty-five minutes at the side of the road, praising the Lord, I started the car as I was due at a business meeting at which I was to preside. Even as I drove down the road, found my way through the city to the meeting place, parked the car, took the elevator, and presided over the business meeting, I was moving in the presence of Jesus which was almost tangible, and all the while I was pouring out my heart in praise. It was only with some difficulty that I got through the meeting, and one man noticed that I had to fight to keep my attention on the business at hand. The visitation of his presence lasted about three hours, and there was an after-aura which lasted about four days. Now all of that is gone but the memory of it. It soon became evident that I was still all too capable of sin, but the experience has definitely changed me. I am not the same person I was before. These changes have to do not only with how I pray, but with my life style. For instance, I still enjoy an occasional game of golf, but I no longer spend every free moment of the Lord's time on the golf course. I also relate to people differently. I am less selfish, more generous, more concerned. And I am deeply convinced of the sin in my life. Neither before nor since have I ever experienced God in any conscious way.

One cannot quickly assess the quality of the experience from the quality of the description. The subjective theological filter may be defective even though the experience is authentic.

2. . . . and its religious significance

Such an experience is by no means limited to the renewal but is unusual in that it is found there in a patterned way.

Note that the focus is on the person of Jesus, not on the Holy Spirit. If the renewal is in any danger it is that of falling into a Jesus cult rather than into a Spirit cult. What emerges is a conviction of the absolute sovereignty of Jesus who is the cosmic Lord.

The primary category is presence. The person experiences that Jesus is real, that he is actual at this moment, that he is now, that he is here, that he cares, and that he moves within that horizon wherein one experiences one's own concrete historical self. With some frequency one hears the astonished discovery: 'He loves me.'

The immediate and unreflective response to presence is praise directed to the majesty of Jesus, to the glory of his sovereign Lordship, to the triumph of his risen victory, to his care. Whatever else may be doubted, it cannot be doubted that he who is worthy of all praise is present.

To be baptised in the Holy Spirit is to be baptised in power. The person is touched by an interior force which changes and transforms, which makes *metanoia* possible. This is authority, command, dominion which touches the heart so that the centre of personal consciousness is given new resources for personal transformation and empowerment for proclamation.

Anyone who has had extensive contact with persons who have claimed to have been baptised in the Spirit knows full well that it does not make them 'instant contemplatives', much less endow them with 'instant perfection'. Nonetheless, a not inconsiderable number of persons experience a short period in which they receive prayer gifts, as did the businessman. The memory of that moment of glorious presence and praise leads many on to a daily regime of prayer and spiritual reading. No one is considered serious about the spiritual life if there is not some schedule of daily prayer. In no way does the experience dispense with discipline, decision, fidelity, effort, asceticism, with all their attendant frustrations. Some have suggested that the total experience in the renewal is too *resurrection-oriented* and *not* sufficiently *cross-centred*. The criticism is frequently justified though there are groups which do not nelect the cross, who insist that *metanoia* starts with repentance and can start nowhere else. Only sinners need a Lord and Saviour; only sinners enter the kingdom.

2. LIFE IN CHRIST

To receive the Spirit is not enough. One must 'walk by the Spirit' (Gal. 5:25). For Paul there are two kinds of Christians: material *(psychikos)* and spiritual *(pneumatikos)*. Both have received the Spirit but the spiritual Christian differs from the material in that he tries to be led by the Spirit, to seek his will and direction in daily decisions.

1. *Having the Courage of one's Emotions*

Frequently the relation of emotion to religious experience is raised. With apologies for referring to my own field research, for years I objected to the emotional content of the experiences related and of the prayer meetings. One day it dawned on me that the emotional level was not high and I had no real foundation for my objections. I was at home with liturgised, formalised expressions of religious sentiment. But if some lay person got up in a prayer meeting and calmly witnessed to what Jesus meant in his life the past week, I felt threatened. I told myself it was all too emotional, and I rejected it. I confused personal with emotional content. This is not to defend every expression in the renewal as devoid of emotional excess. But it should be clear what is under judgment.

Religious experience has to do with the totality of the divine call and the human response. Part of that totality is the emotions. To demand a denatured experience which leaves the emotions completely untouched, would be to settle for what is less threatening; it would also be less human. For most people, as for the businessman, the baptism in the Holy Spirit has some emotional content, which in no way invalidates the experience's authenticity. But for thousands on thousands of other persons the baptism occurred without any perceivable emotional elevation. A deeply personal religious experience is not necessarily a highly emotional one.

2. *Revitalisation of the Sacraments*

For most the involvement in the charismatic renewal is the occasion of a revitalised sacramental life. The best cultic expressions of the renewal are, in my prejudiced judgment, not the prayer meetings but the eucharists. People come together with a real sense of celebration rooted in the presence of the Lord and in commitment to one another. There is a deep sense of praise, and of the sacred, a hunger for the word and for the body and blood. Partly because presence and praise elicits an awareness of sinfulness, the sacrament of reconciliation has been rediscovered as a healing instrument and its worst ritualistic, routinised expressions avoided.

A few react quite differently. Having been exhorted for years to go to confession and to Mass, and, it is claimed, 'nothing happened', they are then led into the baptism in the Spirit, and, in empirical sociological terms, a verifiable transformation takes place. For those involved, a false conclusion is sometimes drawn at this point. These person deduce that the spiritual centre is not in sacramental life but in religious experience, and a false opposition is erected between the two. They feel deceived by the Church which evidently, they claim, did not know where to locate the face of God. To them it must be said that the passionate pursuit of religious experience is an aberration, which has no biblical justification. The true seeker pursues God, not experience.

3. *Charisms as Forms of Service to the Community*

The baptism is central but it is not an adequate description of the experience of the Spirit in the renewal. The Christian life is not one mountain-top experience, nor is it a glorious progress from peak experience to peak experience. Everyone walks by faith in the valleys and has to confront that most disturbing Christian fact: the search for the face of God often ends in the experience of his absence. Any description of the Christian life which omits this builds upon a false enthusiasm. But there may well be moments when the presence breaks through to conscious experience. Baptism in the Spirit seems to belong to the beginning of the Christian life, to initiation, rather than to a later more mature stage. Something of this nature seems to be what Paul is referring to when he asks the Galatians: 'Having *begun* with the Spirit, are you now ending with the flesh? Did you experience so many things in vain?' (3:3, 4). These experiences belong to a different order of religious reality than the great gifts of infused contemplation, raptures and visions. Here experience is spelled with a small 'e'. Though a measure of scepticism is always in order with regard to religious experience (in the first instance charisms are ambiguous and need discernment), one cannot take the norms of mystical theology for the higher personal gifts of prayer and, without qualification, apply them to charisms which are ministries to others.

The renewal emphasises what is clearly Paul's teaching: the Church is entirely ministerial, made up of members in each of whom the Spirit comes to visibility in a charism or service to others. These charisms (prophet, teacher, labour organiser, healer, librarian, sweeper of floors) are directed outward in service to others. All of them belong to the ordinary life of the normal Christian community, which is charismatically constituted because it is an organism of mutually supporting services directed toward building up the body for mission to the world. An outsider quickly learns that all of these are so much a part of normal community life that they receive very little attention. In the more stable communities persons who centre their lives around unusual experiences will be received with some unease and will be considered immature. Service, not experience, is the watchword.

4. *Openness to Social and Political Involvement*

The witness account given above may result in a privatising of some gifts of the Spirit (prophecy, tongues, healing), turning them inward to the little community in an exclusive sectarian sense. But political and social involvement may also be gifts of the Spirit, real experiences of the Spirit's leading and of the presence of Jesus. The charismatic renewal has been severely criticised for its lack of social awareness, and not without justification, but the research shows that those in the renewal are about as much involved in social programmes as the general Catholic population.[2] Generalisations here need careful qualification. In Mexico the charismatic renewal began among those who were already living in the *barrios* with the poor and fully involved in social action programmes. Some South Americans say that the difference is that now they teach the poor to fight against their oppressors while loving and praying for them. Before they had unconsciously taught the poor to hate. This is not a small change.

Behind the sometimes heavy rhetoric of piety is the concern for what in lay terms would be called 'basic Christianity' or what theologians might call 'the core of the Gospel'. The search is for the centre, which is discovered to be relational. Ultimately Christianity has to do with personal and communal relationship to that Lord through whom access in the Spirit is had to the Father. The experience of the gospel takes place where a human person touches a divine person and an ongoing relationship is established. The Father sends the Son; the Spirit leads one to proclaim 'Jesus is Lord'; the risen Jesus baptises in the Holy Spirit who gives access to the Father. Christianity is insertion into that rhythm of relationships from the Father to the Father. In the first instance the gospel is not observance of law, or the acceptance of an ideology. It is not religion but relationship. Essential to the charismatic experience is the insight that the relationship to the divine communion leads to the formation of community, the extension of person to person contact, and the extension of relationship. Pentecost is that point at which the divine communion reaches out beyond itself to form new communions (Acts 4:32).

5. *Open Communities*

Perhaps the most enduring contribution of the renewal is this communitarian aspect. The local community is the primary instrument of evangelisation. What is lacking is not correct techniques of imparting the gospel, but living communities which are so committed to the Lordship of Jesus and to each other that they cause astonishment and wonder. Unless one can point to such already existing communities and say 'If you want to understand what the gospel is, come and see', no effective evangelisation will take place. The living reality carries its own conviction and the gospel becomes believable. This view is so strong in the renewal that it would say: no communities equals no credibility equals no evangelisation.

The re-evaluation of the role of experience brings with it the danger of subjectivism and individualism which in classical Pentecostalism some-times led to the 'Pentecostal star' where there were no checks. Partly to avoid this, spiritual direction and even submission are not uncommon, especially in covenant communities. In these groups everyone including the leaders are under submission to someone else. Group discernment and a system of community decision-making carried out in a prayer context give the strength of mutuality instead of the tyranny of domi-nance.

6. *A Lay Movement*

Though thousands of priests and many bishops and clerical theologians are involved, the renewal has a lay ethos, in the same sense that the New Testament, the gospels in particular, is a lay document. The gospels are not highly sophisticated, refined theological treatises, but *popular reflec-tions* on how the good news was preached in the churches to largely unlettered congregations. By academic standards the gospels are crude, impatient, daring, simple, direct and personal. The use of narrative, doing theology by telling stories, is essentially a lay technique which prefers the graphic and the concrete to the abstract. Jesus as a man of the eyes reflecting on the geography of the countryside (sheep, pigs and fig trees) is another lay habit. His summary of the law in the two commandments of love of God and neighbour (it is almost unnecessary to learn the several hundred precepts of the law) is a typical lay reductionism. Finally, the description by Paul of the process of salvation as a buying back, redemp-tion, is a raw mythological image appealing in its literalness to the lay mind. No mistake should be made. A large part of the New Testament force is to be found in this rough directness, in the metaphors of the usual, in the realism of the ordinary, in crude immediacy. More than that, to sanitise the scriptures of their everyday character, to refine, polish and render elegant would be to defuse them, to kill the surprise with which power and transformation break out of the rough common place.

The renewal has this blunt *popular character* which can be painful for persons theologically trained. Without suggesting that all expressions of the renewal are gross and vulgar, which is patently untrue, it does have a folk character. The clergy and trained theologians, and certain lay persons will want to clean up, tighten up, sharpen and sometimes correct the simplistic use of theological language, the coarse use of scripture, or the enthusiastic expressions of devotion. They must do so with delicacy. The experience of the Spirit in the renewal is in some way tied to clumsy metaphors of the ordinary. To refine the renewal without regard for its populist character would be to deprive it of much of its power to change lives.

Notes

1. See P. Hocken 'The charismatic experience' *The Way,* vol. 18 (1978) pp. 44-55. I am indebted to Peter Hocken for suggested revisions of the present article.

2. See J. Fichter 'Personal comfort and social challenge' *The Catholic Cult of the Paraclete* (New York 1975) pp 80-98.

Jean-René Bouchet

The Discernment of Spirits

THE NEED for discernment which we find more and more frequently in Christian communities seems to be caused by a *growing anxiety* which affects Christians as well as everyone else. Here we do not intend to investigate the old or new causes of this anxiety. We merely note that at the moment even the most solid structures and clear statements are also threatened. Neither theology, liturgy nor even the teaching of the magisterium seems to offer any enlightenment, help or reassurance to those who ask themselves these questions: Who am I? What am I for? What should I do? Am I really where I am?

This need for enlightenment leads Christians to ask for answers from priests or communities who are themselves troubled by a situation for which they are ill prepared. They frequently answer the question by asking others. Often they merely echo the anxiety and uncertainty rather than giving advice. Many bewildered lay folk and priests seek for light elsewhere because they have not found it where they were accustomed to seek. Various sects are notoriously successful with the young. They are seeking life and warmth, communities where they can find light and comfort, masters whose wisdom is passed on by word of mouth, or they sometimes even turn to a well known analyst or guru.

1. DISCERNMENT OF THE GIFTS OF THE SPIRIT

It seems to us that this state of affairs is disappearing. The many studies on discernment of spirits and its conditions and methods is certainly one of the signs of this. The more urgent the need for discernment the more difficult it appears and the more inadequate the experts feel. Hearing confession and giving absolution is easy enough but enlightening, guiding and directing is not. At any rate it is clear that this need for light is found in

103

human hearts, in the inner life of groups and communities. It is also clear that running after gurus and the ideal community are to the spiritual life what violent chemotherapy is to a sickness that ought to be treated by fresh air and exercise.

Discernment of spirits is a spiritual gift that St Paul puts in his list of charismata, that is to say gifts given to one or another member of the community for the good of the body as a whole. But 'spiritual gift' does not mean—or not always—that God gives someone this talent without regard to his 'natural gifts'. We think that spiritual discernment is usually given to men and women who are in the process of reconciliation with themselves, open to the divine life and the logic of the Spirit, gifted with friendly common sense about people and situations, full of good will for the community to which they belong. Of course we know that God's gift can create these attitudes where they did not exist before, but usually, naturally, the opposite is what happens and these attitudes patiently and laboriously learned are the good earth in which the gift of discernment bears good fruit. This is the way with the gifts listed by St Paul: the gift of presiding is given to him who has the 'qualities' of leadership and the gift of teaching to the one who has studied. If this is not so, then someone who receives the gift of teaching must set to work at once to study! But as a spiritual gift is given as a *gift* and is not just the normal development of acquired qualities, it can radically alter a previous hard-won balance. However it does not destroy it. The same is true of discernment. The gift of discernment in the strict sense cannot be taught in any school even if these schools are run by ecclesiastical masters or spiritual directors well trained in the history of spirituality as well as in the most advanced techniques of psychology. But this gift does make use of such acquired qualities as the ability to listen, intuition, delicacy and psychology. It brings a pinch of humour to them. In fact every gift is cultivated to the extent that the receiver is converted to Christ, has had the gospel preached to him, is well educated and at peace with himself.

Thus discernment is perfected in several ways: in the ability to listen with sharp ears, in the ability to be effectively and discreetly *with* the person seeking light, in authentic belonging to the community in which the gift of discernment is to operate. Discernment is never done independently of a community. Of course it is a personal activity but the personal includes the social side both of him who discerns and of him who asks for discernment.

2. GIFTS OF THE INDIVIDUAL AND OF THE COMMUNITY

Within the community the person asked to practise discernment may be the president: thus the tradition of the Church has always accorded the bishop the gift of discernment enabling him to fulfil his presidential ministry fruitfully. If, as unfortunately so often happens, discernment by the community's president seems clumsy or incompetent, this is because it was not accompanied by the power to listen, understanding and community-rootedness which are indispensable to it. It may also happen that the person called to discern has no other function in the Body. This is the case with the people the Russian Orthodox Church calls the *startzi*, and there have also been some and are some in the western church. These 'clairvoyants' have an even greater need to be rooted in the community within which they practise their gift because they are not leaders of it and conflicts can arise between them and the president of the community.

We also speak of community discernment. Here it is a question not of a personal relationship but of a group or community seeking light on a direction to take or a choice to be made. The sign that the decision has been a true exercise of discernment will never be given solely by the unanimity or absolute majority with which it was taken. The decision must also depend on listening to each other and being involved with each other and the relationship with the other communities to which this community is organically linked, the coherence of the direction taken and the fundamental intention of the community. This means that community discernment, like personal discernment, seldom offers guarantees of authenticity. An exercise of discernment is seldom 'evangelically pure' in the sense that a solution can be 'chemically pure'. But this does not ever mean that we are dispensed from trying to engage in both community and personal discernment. If these exercises in discernment bear fruits of discord or sadness, the opposite to the fruits spoken of by St Paul (Gal. 5:22), they will not be in accordance with the gospel. We judge the spiritual authenticity of discernment by its fruits.

3. DISCERNMENT AS PROCLAMATION OF THE GOSPEL

Discernment in the strict sense is distinguised from other seekings for light by its gospel tone. For him who discerns and for him who seeks discernment, as for the community which engages in community discernment, it is not a question of eliminating stress, abolishing conflicts or tensions, nor even having for a goal the acquiring of personal or communal psychological health, which as we know can go together with a true spiritual desert. Fundamentally discernment is a particular kind of proclamation of the gospel. But is this not the case with all spiritual gifts?

Etymologically discernment means sorting. This is how the old monks saw it. This is what Cassian is thinking about when he compares the discerner with the money changer who sorts out the genuine money from the false. It is a question of 'sorting out spirits' and at present, when spirits noisily abound, it is an important task. But is not the best way of sorting out spirits still to serve the Spirit of light present in our hearts and in the group that tries to follow his guidance?

In this sense the gift of discernment at its best is the proclamation of the Good News which brings light, warmth and fruitfulness, by a man or woman who humbly and truly tries to live by it, to men and women who want to receive it into their lives and let it transform them. In the community discernment means preparing the way for this Good News so that it can spread freely and bear good sound fruit. That is to say that discernment as clairvoyance is for the service of life and if it is expressed by word it is listening and not power. 'Listen brother, or rather listen to Christ, or better still, let us listen to him together . . .' 'If you like . . .' Discernment advises, invites, arouses but never imposes. It can be expressed forcefully, it may even be a denunciation but its aim is always constructive. It serves the whole Body, it is ordained for this service and this is what distinguishes it from every other 'helping relationship'. It is not a substitute for them. However it can pass judgment on these other 'helping relationships': some it will agree with, some not.

The gift of discernment is the service of light by the annunciation of light, light which is life.

> 'And the life was the light of men.
> The light shines in the darkness
> and the darkness has not overcome it . . .
> There was a man sent from God,
> whose name was John.
> He came for testimony,
> to bear witness to the light,
> that all might believe through him.
> He was not the light,
> but came to bear witness to the light.'

(John 1:4-8)

Translated by Dinah Livingstone

Ivan Panchovski

An Orthodox View

1. SOME PNEUMATOLOGICAL FUNDAMENTALS OF ORTHODOXY

1. *The Presence of the Spirit*

As in all the other Christian denominations, there is in Eastern
Orthodoxy a great desire for the Holy Spirit. Accordingly the Orthodox
believer, from inner prompting and in obedience to the apostle's instruction (Eph. 5:18), prays daily, in the liturgy and privately, in words which
have come down from the most ancient times: 'Βασιλεῦ οὐράνιε,
heavenly king, let the Paraclete come to us and dwell in us to cleanse us
from all guilt and sin and to save our souls.' The Holy Spirit, as a divine
hypostasis, is in fact present everywhere (see Ps. 139:7-13), and fills all
things, but the believer longs to live in personal communion with him and
to receive life-giving, sanctifying and saving gifts. Not only Jesus Christ,
but also the Holy Spirit, who bears witness to the saviour (John 15:26), is
present in the Church of God, intercedes for the faithful with sighs too
deep for words, helps them in their weakness (Rom. 8:26-27) and pours
out on them the lavish and infinitely various grace of God.

The gifts of the Holy Spirit were particularly clearly visible in the
primitive Church. The presence of the Paraclete in the Church, his
wonderful action and his diverse gifts could be seen not only by the
faithful but also by unbelievers, even by Simon Magus (Acts 8:9ff.).
Charisms or spiritual gifts were a typical feature of the life of the primitive
Church. The enthusiastic, unusual and extraordinary spiritual gifts are
particularly striking in the detailed lists of charisms (Rom. 12:6ff.; 1 Cor.
12:8ff.). But it is a historical fact that after the apostolic age and even
towards its end these charisms became increasingly rare and appeared
only sporadically and for short periods. Nevertheless this fact does not
mean that the early Church lost its pneumatic dimension and no longer

offered believers fellowship in the Holy Spirit, that charisms completely died out in it. In accordance with the changed needs and new tasks of the Church other charisms took precedence in the post-apostolic period. The charismatic element is thus part of the essence of the Church and continues to be active in it, not just through ministries and sacraments, but also through a constant succession of new forms of witness, confession, martyrdom and service to neighbour, to one's own people and to the whole human race. In this sense the saints, the martyrs, the confessors, the fathers of the Church and many other pious and virtuous Christians, are charismatics.

Since the purpose of this article is to give an Orthodox view of the present charismatic movement, it is to the point to mention first that a distinct charismatic movement does not at present exist in the Orthodox Church. Nevertheless the Holy Spirit has been a living reality in the Orthodox Church from the beginning, and pneumatology an important concern of its theology.

2. *Spirit and Sacrament*

In the liturgy of St John Chrysostom, which is the one most frequently celebrated in the Orthodox Churches, the living and glorified Lord and the Holy Spirit are indissolubly linked in the eucharist. During the consecration the eucharistic gifts are transformed into the body and blood of Christ through the Holy Spirit. Consequently the Christian at communion receives the Lord and the Holy Spirit simultaneously. In an ancient anaphora of John Chrysostom the congregation asks for the descent of the Holy Spirit on the gifts and on the community of the faithful: 'We call upon you, we pray you and implore you to send your Holy Spirit down on us and these gifts and make this bread the precious body of your Christ and this drink the precious blood of your Christ. Transform them through your Holy Spirit, that they may bring all who partake of them unity of soul, forgiveness of sins, fellowship with your Holy Spirit, the fullness of the kingdom, salvation from you and not judgment or damnation.'

The Holy Spirit is also present and active in other sacraments of the Orthodox Church. Their sacramental nature and action depends on the Holy Spirit. To substantiate this I will limit myself to a small number of sacramental prayers. At baptism the water is sanctified by the Holy Spirit. In a baptismal preface the priest asks that God may renew the candidate to new life and fill him with the power of the Holy Spirit. In the Orthodox rite of confirmation the oil is consecrated by the descent of the Holy Spirit. The minister then anoints the confirmand with chrism and says, 'Be sealed by the gift of the Holy Spirit'. The confirmand thus receives the sign of the Holy Spirit and from now on is under the guidance of this divine person. Through the sacrament of order a person receives a special enduring charism. The Holy Spirit appoints the priest or bishop as an overseer to care for the Church of God (Acts 20:28). The preface for the ordination of a priest asks for the descent of the grace of the Holy Spirit. In the Orthodox rite of the anointing of the sick the Church asks for the oil to be blessed, for the Holy Spirit to be sent down on it and for the oil to be filled with the healing power of the Holy Spirit. It goes on to ask that the Holy Spirit may descend on the sick person for the healing of the body, the forgiveness of sins and the salvation of the soul. We may also mention here the prayer in which the Church during the eucharist begs for the help, grace and gift of the Holy Spirit at the beginning of any work.

2. AN ANALYTIC ASSESSMENT OF THE CHARISMATIC MOVEMENT

1. *Postive Aspects*

As an Orthodox theologian I can see positive sides to the present-day charismatic movement. Its aim of turning to the Holy Spirit, who is rightly described as the living breath of the Church and the driving force of Church life, reflects a real need in Christianity today. The experience of the Spirit in the charismatic movement is also bringing about a renewal of the spiritual life in the Church where it has attached too much importance to its human side, its sociological structure, institutional dimension and historical tradition. There are also obvious effects or fruits of the Spirit in the charismatic movement. The sense of the presence and closeness of God becomes keener, trust in God firmer, faith deeper, prayer more fervent, devotion more spontaneous, study of holy scripture more active, witness more successful, fellowship more fraternal, service of neighbour more committed and ecumenical contacts more enriching on each side. In direct contact with the charismatic movement one feels an elevated spiritual atmosphere similar to that of the community of the saints in the primitive Church. The charismatic movement can really be described as a religious awakening and a revolution in the life of the established churches which will contribute to a renewal of the Church and the world.

2. *Negative Aspects*

On the other hand I also find some weaknesses and dangers in the charismatic movement, which have also been pointed out by people active in the movement and by observers in the West.

(a) In terms of the psychology of religion the charismatic movement displays an excessive emphasis on emotion. This excess of emotion in quite a few charismatic groups is also combined with a deep mistrust of

thinking in general. Emotion is important in all religions, including Christianity, but it must not be isolated from the content of the historical revelation. If it is, Christian religious feeling can turn into a mere emotional state and an empty spiritualism. The Christian faith takes over the whole person and makes demands on all his or her mental and physical powers. Jesus and the apostles call for worship 'in spirit and truth' (John 4:24; 1 Cor. 5:8) and 'rational worship' (Rom. 12:1). Christian faith is expressed in the doing of the heavenly Father's will (Matt. 7:21) and is active in love (Gal. 5:6). The apostle Paul warns not just the charismatics of Corinth but also the charismatics of today not to despise thinking and to become mature in thinking (1 Cor. 14:20).

(b) Like all mystical movements, the charismatic movement shows a latent, and sometimes even obvious, tendency to substitute personal experience for scriptural revelation and the study of doctrine. This tendency derives from the immediacy of individual experience and personal certainty about its promptings. It can lead to a situation in which convictions obtained through mystical or charismatic experience are treated as norms, from which it is easy to slip into a cult of ecstasy. The gift of prophecy is particularly liable to the temptation of ecstasy. Fidelity to holy scripture is the surest guarantee against this temptation, since apart from scripture there is no other Gospel (see Gal. 1:7ff.). Only scripture gives instruction in salvation through faith in Jesus Christ (2 Tim. 3:15). The Orthodox Church also regards the tradition which comes down from the apostles as a source of revealed truths. New truths can be revealed through the charism of prophecy which is active in the Church but, in comparison with the truths of scripture, they have only limited validity, for an individual or a particular group.

(c) It is the phenomenon of glossolalia in the charismatic movement which provokes the strongest reservations. 'Speaking in tongues' has a privileged place in the movement. It is regarded as a mark of the outpouring of the Spirit, a proof of real 'baptism in the Spirit' and a way of obtaining other gifts. Consequently all 'believers baptised in the Spirit' are expected to speak in tongues daily in their prayers. There are even demands for speaking in tongues to be the normal experience of all Christians. In the Orthodox view glossolalia is not a characteristic of the primitive Church alone; it can reappear in any age. Nevertheless even without it the Holy Spirit can be present in a Christian and working for his or her sanctification. At the same time it is important to mention that glossolalia also exist in natural religions and can even be provoked chemically and psychologically. Well-known psychiatrists and psychotherapists attribute most experiences of glossolalia to an action of the unconscious as a result of a 'regression of the ego'. Even Christian charismatics regard speaking in tongues as a natural gift which can also be

used by demonic forces. Glossolalia can therefore be a danger to Christian spiritual life. As a result of these discussions great care is very rightly recommended in dealing with glossolalia. The gift of speaking in tongues should neither be completely denied and opposed nor extravagantly praised, let alone insisted on. Its practice brings very little benefit to the individual's spiritual life and its lack is no obstacle to striving for salvation and being saved.

(d) Fascination with charisms could lead to a disparagement of non-charismatic Christians, to a separation from the mother Church and the formation of small conventicles, new denominations, a charismatic higher or spiritual church. It is currently being said that there is a serious danger that the charismatic movement in England and Scotland will become a 'house church movement' outside the Church. But the will of God is that all Christians should be one (John 17:20). The charismatic movement has a tendency to cause new splits and divisions in the Church. There are reports that some communities are being fragmented and torn to pieces by charismatic enthusiasts—but the Holy Spirit is a force for unity (see 1 Cor. 12:13)!

3. CRITERIA FOR THE DISCERNMENT OF SPIRITS

Experience of the Spirit is the basic experience in the charismatic movement. In the Neo-Pentecostalist movement charismatic experience in the most important thing—it is everything. But how is the genuineness of charismatic experience to be determined? Even with what seem outwardly the most reliable experiences there may be weeds mixed with the wheat. Prudence and testing are therefore essential (see 1 John 4:1). The gift of 'discernment of spirits' (1 Cor. 12:10) does not work automatically, but on principles some of which come from the Holy Spirit himself while others are learned by experienced community leaders, ministers and laity. The following criteria for the discernment of spirits is based on holy Scripture, the tradition of the saints and the spiritual experience of the Church.

First, the charismatic experience must start from faith in Jesus Christ and contain a direct or indirect confession of this faith (see 1 John 4:2-3). The Paraclete, the spirit of truth, is sent to believers by Jesus Christ to lead them still further into the fullness of his truth; he glorifies Jesus because what he declares to Christians he takes from Jesus' fullness (John 16:7, 13-14). So no-one who speaks in the Spirit of God can say 'Jesus be cursed!' and no-one can say 'Jesus is Lord', except in the Holy Spirit (1 Cor. 12:3).

Second, the content of the charismatic experience must agree with the revelations contained in the scriptures and traditions inspired by the Holy Spirit. In all revelations of the Holy Spirit there is unity, continuity and consistency; they contain no contradictions.

Third, spiritual gifts are allotted to believers *in the Church* (see 1 Cor. 12:28). The Church is the mysterious body of the Lord in which everything is made alive and holy by the Holy Spirit. The various gifts of the Holy Spirit are given to equip the saints for the building up of the mystical body of Christ (Eph. 4:12). There may be many defects in the empirical structure of the Church, but it remains nonetheless a divine and human organism in which we can attain sanctification and salvation. Only in the maternal and gracious bosom of the Church can the baptised Christian grow properly and reach the measure of the stature of the fullness of Christ (see Eph. 4:13). Accordingly all Christians, including charismatics, are required to belong to the Church and to be obedient to it (see Matt. 18:17).

Fourth, service to the community, to neighbour, to mankind, is a mark of the spiritual charisms. According to the teaching of the apostles, charisms are gifts for service, given for the benefit of the community, to build it up (1 Cor. 12:4-7; 14:4, 12), for mutual service and not for individual advantage and private enjoyment.

Fifth, genuine striving to preserve the *unity* of the community and of the whole Church and to maintain the fraternal fellowship of its members is a mark of the person who is filled with the Holy Spirit, since the Spirit is a Spirit of unity and fellowship. Dissension and division among Christians mean that they are still of the flesh and behaving in a human way (1 Cor. 1:10; 3:3).

Sixth, the Lord's advice to judge a tree by its fruits (Matt. 7:16ff.; Luke 6:43-44) gives us an infallible criterion for the discernment of spirits. The 'fruits of the Spirit' listed by the apostle Paul (Gal. 5:22-23) are also irrefutable evidence for the divine origin and nature of spiritual gifts.

Seven, the *agape* which the apostle Paul mentions first among the fruits of the Spirit (Gal. 5:22) is further infallible criterion for the discernment of spirits. *Agape* is part of the essence of the Christian character and life (John 13:35). Without it no spiritual gift has any value or brings any benefit (1 Cor. 13: 1-3).

Eight, humility is an additional mark of the possession of a spiritual gift, because 'God opposes the proud, but gives grace to the humble' (James 4:6).

These criteria could, of course, be expanded, or others added, but I believe that they are sufficient as they stand for a proper discernment of spirits. In attempting discernment it is advisable to beware of hasty judgments, to avoid making a disastrous mistake and saying a word against the Holy Spirit which will not be forgiven either in this world or the world to come (Matt. 12:32). In unclear and complicated cases, when some spiritual gifts are beyond our power of judgment and we are not in a position to reach a wise judgment, it is better to practise tolerance, as the Lord advises (Matt. 13:29-30).

Today all Christian denominations emphasise the role of the Holy Spirit in the world, in history and in the Church. The Holy Spirit is present and at work among Christians and among all men, but he never destroys human *freedom* or does violence to human will. That is why the apostle Paul appeals to Christians not to extinguish the Spirit (1 Thess. 5:19) but to keep alive the gifts of God which are within them (2 Tim. 1:6). The constant growth of the spiritual gifts given to Christians will produce a lasting renewal.

Translated by Francis McDonagh

Hans Küng

Epilogue:
How should we speak today
about the Holy Spirit?

IS THE Holy Spirit the Great Unknown? Is everything that we can say about the Holy Spirit really as disparate as it would seem to be at first sight? To some extent there is bound to be a difference if the person who is speaking about the Holy Spirit is a Catholic, an Orthodox, a Lutheran, a Reformed or a Free Church Christian or if he considers the Holy Spirit from the point of view of biblical theology or the history of dogma or from a confessional, institutional or spiritual standpoint.

It is true, of course, that there are clear dangers in this Review of a confessional one-sidedness and a partisan approach in theology and many of the authors are equally clearly critically aware of these dangers. There are dangers, for example, of irrelevant speculation about the Son and the Spirit in Eastern and especially in Western theology. There are dangers of a formalisation in the relationship between the Word and the Spirit in the theology of the Reformed Church and even more particularly in that of the Lutheran Church. There are dangers of ideology in the case of the Spirit in the Catholic understanding of office and especially in the Roman Catholic understanding. There are many other dangers, including that of an over-emotional approach towards the Spirit in the charismatic movement.

It is neither desirable nor possible to go into individual details here. What has, however, to be done in this concluding editorial summary is to emphasise that, despite all the differences in approach, there is only one Spirit. That Spirit is both the Spirit of God and the Spirit of Jesus Christ and he is active in the world, in the Church and in individual believers.

114

The pressing question that is being asked today, not only by theologians, but also by very many pastoral workers and lay people, is: How is it possible to speak intelligibly nowadays about this one Holy Spirit?

Can I venture to provide a brief, elementary and universally intelligible answer to this elementary question? I will try to do so, not by summarising or systematically elaborating the different aspects that have been stressed in the various contributions, but rather by suggesting a possible way of speaking responsibly about the Holy Spirit today.

What, then, does 'Spirit' mean? Tangible and yet intangible, invisible and yet powerful, as real as the air that is full of energy, the wind, the storm, as important to life as the air we breathe—these images have all been used by ancient man to represent the 'Spirit' and the invisible activity of God. 'Spirit'—in Hebrew *ruah,* in Greek *pneuma*—is, according to the beginning of the story of creation, the 'wind' or 'storm' of God that moved over the waters. 'Spirit' in the biblical sense is contrasted with 'flesh' or the created reality that is corruptible and means the power or strength that proceeds from God. It is the invisible power and strength of God that was creatively or destructively active, giving life or condemning to death, in the creation of the world and man in the history of salvation and especially that of Israel. The same Spirit has continued to be active in the Church, powerfully or gently seizing hold of men, transporting individuals or groups into ecstasy and frequently present in extraordinary phenomena, in great men and women, in Moses and the Judges of Israel, in warriors, singers, kings, prophets and prophetesses.

What does 'Holy Spirit' mean? Although it is quite possible to claim, on the basis of the word alone, that the Holy Spirit is the spirit of man, it is not. The Holy Spirit is the Spirit of God, distinguished as the *holy* Spirit from the unholy spirit of man and his world. In the New Testament sense, this Spirit is not, as it often has been in the history of comparative religions, a magical, substantial, mysteriously supernatural fluid with dynamic powers, nor is it a magic being of an animistic kind. On the contrary, the Holy Spirit is none other than God himself! He is God himself in his closeness to man and the world as the one who seizes hold of man but cannot be seized, the one who gives but is not at man's disposal, the one who creates life but also judges. The Holy Spirit is therefore not a third party or a thing between God and man, but God's personal closeness to man.

What does believing in the Holy Spirit mean? It means a simple and trusting acceptance that God himself can be inwardly present for me in faith and that he can, as a power conferring grace, gain control of me in my innermost self and in my heart. I can therefore in faith trust that the Spirit of God is not a spirit that enslaves. He is none other than the Spirit of Jesus Christ who was taken up to and received by God. He is the Spirit, then, of Jesus Christ himself. And because Jesus is the one who was taken up to and received by God, he is, in the Spirit, the living Lord and as such normative for individual Christians and for the community of believers as a whole. On the basis of this concrete norm, I can also test and discern the spirits and know that no hierarchy, no theology and no enthusiasm that seeks to appeal to the Holy Spirit while at the same time disregarding Jesus, his word and his life and behaviour can really be appealing to the Spirit of Jesus Christ. It is at this point clearly that we reach the limits of all obedience, consent and cooperation.

Believing in the Holy Spirit or the Spirit of God and Jesus Christ means knowing—and this is particularly important nowadays in view of the many charismatic and pneumatic activities that are taking place—that the Spirit is never my own potential, but always God's power and gift. The Spirit is not an unholy spirit of man, a spirit of the age, a spirit of the Church, a spirit of the Church's office or a spirit of enthusiasm, but always the holy Spirit of God who blows where he will and who cannot be claimed as a justification of any absolute power to teach or to govern or of any unfounded dogmatic theology, any pious fanaticism or any false certainty of faith. No one—no bishop, no professional theologian, no parish priest and no lay person—can ever 'possess' the Spirit, but everyone can ask again and again to receive the Spirit.

Receiving the Holy Spirit, then, is not a magical event that I allow to happen to me. It is opening myself inwardly to the message of God and therefore to God himself and his crucified Christ and in this way letting myself be seized by the Spirit of God and his Christ. Believing in the Holy Spirit, in the Spirit of God and Jesus Christ, also means believing in the Spirit of freedom. As Paul said, where the Spirit of God is, there is freedom. This freedom is a freedom from guilt, the law and death. It is a freedom in the world and the Church, a freedom to act, to love and to live in peace, justice, hope and thankfulness. This freedom in the Spirit can also prevail despite all opposition and compulsion in society and the Church and despite all human failure and imperfection.

In this freedom given by the Spirit too, I and countless other unknown men and women can find new courage, comfort and strength again and again in all the great and the small decisions, fears, danger, premonitions and expectations of life. The Spirit of freedom in this way acts as the Spirit of the future and points to the way ahead—not to a hereafter of consolation, but to an involvement in the present, in everyday experience in the world until its fulfilment, for which we have a pledge in the Spirit.

Father, Son and Spirit—there is a correct relationship between God, Jesus (the Son, the Word, Christ) and the Spirit which demonstrates both the real distinction and the undivided unity that exist between them. Modern man is not always helped in his understanding of this relationship by the interpretations that are based on ancient, hellenistic ways of thinking and the dogmatic pronouncements that have been formulated in this tradition. Like all such statements, they are historically conditioned and cannot be simply identified with the biblical accounts. They can therefore neither be thoughtlessly rejected nor unreflectingly repeated. They have rather to be differently interpreted for modern man on the basis of the New Testament.

God revealed himself through the Son in the Spirit. It is important to think of the unity of the Father, Son and Spirit as an event of revelation that is at the same time a unity of revelation. If this is done, we have to be careful not to question the unity and the singleness of God, not to do away with the different 'roles' of the Father, the Son and the Spirit, not to reverse the sequence of the three and especially not to forget for one moment Jesus' humanity.

It is, in fact, from the Christological question that the Trinitarian question has developed. The relationship between God and Jesus has to be considered with reference to the Spirit. A Christology without a Pneumatology or doctrine of the Holy Spirit would be an incomplete Christology. We can express this idea unhesitatingly: As God's Son, the true man Jesus of Nazareth is the real revelation of the one true God, but immediately afterwards we have to ask: How is Jesus present for us? The answer to this question is: He is not physically or materially present, but he is also not unreally present. He is present in the Spirit, in the mode of existence of the Spirit, as a spiritual reality. The Spirit is the presence of God and of the risen Christ for individual believers and for the community of the Church. In this sense, God himself is revealed through Jesus Christ in the Spirit.

Translated by David Smith

Contributors

JEAN-RENÉ BOUCHET was born in 1936 and is a Dominican of the Province of Toulouse. He was ordained priest in 1966. From 1967-72 he was professor of patristics at Toulouse, from 1972-76 he was master of novices and at present he is prior of the Dominican Monastery at Strasbourg. He is the director of 'La Vie Spirituelle'. His publications include: *Le vocabulaire de l'union des natures chez St Gregoire de Nysse* (1968); *Le renouveau charismatique interpellée* (with others) (Paris 1977).

MICHAEL FAHEY, SJ, was born in 1933 and is professor of ecclesiology and director of graduate studies in the Department of Theological Studies, Concordia University, Montreal, Canada. Since 1970 he has been a consultant theologian for the Orthodox/Roman Catholic Bilateral Consultation in America of which he is now Executive Secretary. He is author of *Cyprian and the Bible* (Tübingen 1971) and co-author with J. Meyendorff of *Trinitarian Theology East and West* (Brookline, Mass. 1977). He has published widely in the area of ecclesiology and ecumenism in *Theological Studies, Diakonia, Het Christelijk Oosten, Journal of Ecumenical Studies, The Jurist*, etc.

ALEXANDRE GANOCZY was born in Budapest in 1928. He studied at the Pazmany University in Budapest, at the Institut Catholique de Paris and at the Papal Gregorian University. He is Professor of Systematic Theology at the University of Würzburg. He has published various essays and several books including, among others, *Le jeune Calven* (Wiesbaden 1966); *Ecclesia ministrans* (Freiburg i. Br. 1968); *Sprechen von Gott in heutiger Gesellschaft* (Freiburg i. Br. 1974); *Der schöpferische Mensch und die Schöpfung Gottes* (Mainz 1976); and *Einführung in die katholische Sakramentenlehre* (Darmstadt 1979).

HERMANN HÄRING was born in 1937, graduated in philosophy (Munich) and theology (Tübingen) and specialised in dogmatic and ecumenical theology in Tübingen. He works at present for the Institute for Ecumenical Research at the University of Tübingen. His most recent publication is *Die Macht des Bösen. I. Das Erbe Augustins* (Ökumenische Theologie 3, Zürich 1979).

INGE LØNNING was born in Bergen, Norway, in 1938. He studied philology and theology in Bergen and Oslo and served as a pastor in the Lutheran Church of Norway between 1964 and 1965, when he left on being awarded a grant to do theological research in Oslo and Tübingen. Since 1971, he has been Professor of Systematic Theology at Oslo University. His publications include 'Paulus und Petrus, Gal. 2. 11 ff, als kontroverstheologisches Fundamentalproblem' *Studia Theologica* (1970) pp. 1-69, and *'Kanon im Kanon', Zum dogmatischen Grundlagenproblem des neutestamentlichen Kanons*, 1972. He is also the editor of the Norwegian monthly journal *Kirke og Kultur*.

KILIAN McDONNELL, OSB, was born in Great Falls, Montana, USA. He is founder and President of the Institute for Ecumenical and Cultural Research and Professor of Theology at St John's University, both at Collegeville, Minnesota. Among his publications are *John Calvin, the Church and the Eucharist* (Princeton University Press, 1967); *Charismatic Renewal and the Churches* (Seabury, New York, 1976); *Charismatic Renewal and Ecumenism* (Paulist Press, New York, 1978). He has been active ecumenically in bi-lateral dialogues at both the national and international levels.

HARDING MEYER was born in 1928 in Hardingen, Germany, into an Evangelical-Lutheran family. Since 1971 he has been Research Professor at the Institute for Ecumenical Research in Strasbourg. His publications include the following: *Das Wort Pius IX: 'Die Tradition bin ich'— Päpstliche Unfehlbarkeit und apostolische Traditionen in den Debatten und Dekreten des Vaticanum I* (1965); *Luthertum und Katholizismus in Gespräch—Ergebnisse und Stand der katholisch/lutherischen Gespräche* (1973). He is also editor of *Ökumenische Perspektiven* and *Ökumenische Dokumentation*.

BATTISTA MONDIN was born in 1926 at Monte di Male (Vicenza), and became a priest in the Congregation of the Saverian Fathers. He has studied the philosophy of history at Harvard as well as philosophy and theology in his native country. He attended Vatican II as a *peritus* and is now Professor of Medieval Philosophy and Philosophical Anthropology at the Pontifical Urban University, Director of the Institute for the Study of Atheism at the same university, and Consultor at the Sacred Congregation for the Clergy. He is a regular contributor to the *Osservatore Romano,* as well as to many philosophical and theological journals, both in Italy and abroad. He has written several hundred articles, and more than thirty books, among them the following: *The Principle of Analogy in Protestant and Catholic Theology* (The Hague 1968); *L'Umo. Chi è?* (Milan 1977); *I grandi teologi del secolo XX* (Turin 1972); *Il problema del linguaggio teologico dalle origini ad oggi* (Brescia 1975); *Le teologie del nostro tempo* (Rome 1975); *Le cristologie moderne* (Rome 1979); *I teologi della liberazione* (Rome 1977).

IVAN PANCHOVSKI was born in 1913 in Oboriste (Bulgaria). He studied theology and philosophy in Sofia, Berlin, Leipzig and Jena, where he gained a PhD. Since 1961 he has been Professor of Systematic Theology at the Religious Academy in Sofia. He has written many books on religion and science and on ethics, most recently *Christliche Liebe zu Gott* (1972); *Die christliche Selbstliebe* (1972); *Die Ethik der christlichen Liebe* (1973); *Christliche Nächstenliebe* (1977); *Kants Ethik mit Rücksicht auf ihre Einstellung zur Religion* (1978).

DIETRICH RITSCHL was born in 1929 in Basle, Switzerland. He has been a curate in Basel-Land and pastor in Edinburgh. He has taught patristics and systematic theology at Austin, Texas; Pittsburgh, Pennsylvania; and Union Seminary, New York between 1957 and 1970. He has had visiting professorships at Melbourne, Australia, and Dunedin, New Zealand, in 1970, 1972, 1974, 1977, and 1979, and at Houston, Texas, and he has lectured in Eastern Europe, in Asia, and in England and Scotland. From 1970 onwards he has been Professor of Systematic Theology and Ethics at Mainz University. His publications include: *Vom Leben in der Kirche* (Neukirchen, 1957) (E.T. *Christ Our Life,* Edinburgh 1960); *Athanasius, Versuch einer Interpretation* (Zürich 1964); *Memory and Hope: An Inquiry Concerning the Presence of Christ* (New York 1967); *'Story' als Rohmaterial der Theologie* (Zürich 1976); *Konzepte, Band I: Gesammelte Aufsätze, Patristische Studien* (Berne 1976) and articles in various periodicals.

EDUARD SCHWEIZER was born in Basle in 1913. He studied at the Universities of Basle, Marburg and Zürich, under K. Barth, R. Bultmann and E. Brunner, and he holds honorary doctorates from Mainz, Vienna, St Andrews and Melbourne. Since 1949 he has been Professor of New Testament in Zürich. He has published several books on New Testament subjects, and written numerous scholarly essays in German and English. He is also the author of several articles in Kittel's *Theologisches Wörterbuch zum Neuen Testament.*

THEODORE STYLIANOPOULOS is Professor of New Testament and Eastern Orthodox Spirituality at Hellenic College and Holy Cross Greek Orthodox School of Theology in Brookline, Mass. USA. Born in Messinia, Greece in 1937, he emigrated to the United States (1951) where he received his major education, taking theological degrees at Holy Cross, Boston University School of Theology and Harvard Divinity School. His graduate theological degrees are in New Testament and Early Christian Literature. He has published a book *Justin Martyr and the Mosaic Law* (Missoula 1975) and many articles in various journals. Teaching at Hellenic College and Holy Cross since 1967, he has also served as a parish priest in the Boston area during 1965-76. He is a member of the Orthodox-Roman Catholic Consultation in the United States.

JOHN H. YODER's work on reformation history began with his Basle dissertation *Die Gespräche zwischen Täufern und Reformatoren in der Schweiz* (Karlsruhe 1962), continued in *Täufertum und Reformation im Gespräch* (Zurich 1968). In 1974-75 he was visiting professor of Church history in the faculty of Protestant theology in the University of Strasbourg. Between 1955 and 1975 he frequently represented the North American Mennonite community in ecumenical meetings. In the field of social ethics he has published *The Politics of Jesus* (Grand Rapids 1962) and *The Original Revolution* (Scottdale 1972). He is Professor of Theology at the University of Notre Dame and at the Associated Mennonite Biblical Seminaries.